LAURA ASHLEY BEDROOMS

LAURA ASHLEY
BEDROOMS

SUSAN IRVINE

HARMONY BOOKS

New York

Published in the United States by Harmony Books, a
division of Crown Publishers, Inc., 225 Park Avenue
South, New York, New York 10003 and represented in
Canada by the Canadian MANDA Group

Published in Great Britain by George Weidenfeld &
Nicolson Limited, 91 Clapham High Street, London
SW4 7TA, England

Laura Ashley and logo are trademarks of Laura Ashley
Manufacturing BV.

HARMONY and colophon are trademarks of Crown
Publishers, Inc.

Manufactured in Italy

Library of Congress Cataloging-in-Publication Data
Irvine, Susan.
    Laura Ashley bedrooms.
    Bibliography: p.
    Includes index.
    1. Bedrooms.   2. Interior decoration.   3.   Laura
Ashley (Firm)   I. Title
NK2117.B4178 1988   747.7′7   87–23613
ISBN 0–517–56759–8
10 9 8 7 6 5 4 3 2 1

First Edition

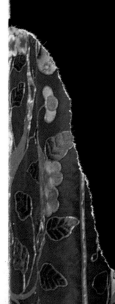

CONTENTS

INTRODUCTION

This is a book of ideas, to be browsed through rather than followed to the letter. It looks at the decorative possibilities of the bedroom, and discusses the elements of colour, pattern, fabrics and furnishings which will evoke different moods. What it does not tell you is how many yards of chintz you will need and where to put the stitches.

Many of the bedrooms in the book have been decorated using the Laura Ashley Home Furnishing and the Laura Ashley Decorator Collections. The sheer diversity of Laura Ashley in recent years, always within a particularly English sense of style, will come as a surprise to many readers. We are all familiar with the classic country sprigs and country freshness, but rather more unexpected are the splendid country-house master prints or the Bohemian whimsy of the Omega workshop reproductions.

The book is divided into chapters, the first of which is a brief history of how the bedroom looked and how it would be used from the Dark Ages to the present day. The next chapter focuses on the bed itself and how pillows, cushions, covers, canopies and bedheads can all change its character. This is followed by the core of the book, a series of chapters each devoted to a particular style of bedroom, be it rustic, country-house, romantic, period or modern town-house. Each chapter is broken up into sections, first trying to capture the feel of the style, then looking at where it springs from and then how to create it yourself, starting with wallpapers, fabric, paint and decorative details through to the furniture and the bed itself. Again, the aim is to inspire. The chapter on the period bedroom is dealt with slightly differently, with five period re-creations, each showing how a bedroom might have looked at that particular period.

Above all, this book is intended as a pleasure in itself. The bedroom provides unique decorative possibilities; hopefully this will be a spur to your imagination.

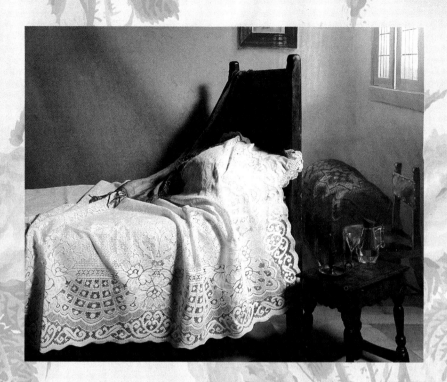

Acknowledgments

My grateful thanks are due to Ian de Castello-Cortes for his pithy and swiftly despatched research, and immense help in editing; to Ann, Gordon and Karen Irvine for providing a vast featherbed, rustic-style, in the wilds of Scotland; to Katherine Jeffery at Laura Ashley for absolutely everything; to Sally Gritten, Brian Jones and Pauline Griffiths at Laura Ashley for enlightening me on the background to the fabrics, and to Suzy Baring for uncomplaining help with picture details; to Jan Croot for picture research; to David Roos for his lovely illustrations; and above all to my constant mentor, Denny Hemming at Weidenfelds for orchestrating the project with inventiveness and firm judgment, and to her sorcerer's apprentice, Lucy Baxter.

A HISTORY
OF THE
BEDCHAMBER

We ourselves have lain full oft upon straw pallets covered onlie with a sheet, or rough mats, and a good rounde log under our heads instead of a boulster ... Then, if the goodman of the house had within seven years of his marriage a mattress or a flock bed and thereto a stack of chaff to rest his head on, he thought himself to be as well-lodged as the lord of the town.
Parson Harrison, reminiscing on the middling bed of
Tudor England

A Glance at the Ancients

Whilst our ancestors slept on piles of skins and moss not far removed from a hedgehog's heap of leaves, the Ancients were reclining on beds of legendary splendour. We hear of kings in the Old Testament lounging on 'beds . . . of gold and silver upon a pavement of . . . marble', and of the bronze beds of Assyrian potentates bristling with precious stones. The tombs of the Pharaohs revealed couches of ebony, chased gold and ivory with feline feet, or footboards in the shape of fabulous composite animals (they never had headboards as these were thought to encroach on the seat of the soul). Instead of a soft pillow, the Egyptians rested their heads on a hard semi-cylindrical bolster of stone or metal, a common preference of early civilizations.

For the Greeks and Romans the bed was the focus of social life. A Greek *kline* (from which we get the word 'recline') was a slim, elegant couch with a low headrest that was used for eating, for holding forth, and for sleeping. It was softer than its Egyptian equivalent, with a thin, sparsely stuffed mattress. Blankets were used for warmth, though some sources indicate that the Athenians simply wrapped themselves by night in the versatile length of cloth that became their clothes by day; and they piled soft cushions under their feet as well as their heads. The Romans had more luxurious tastes, with silk coverlets and feather mattresses. But these early civilizations seem like a distant dream. Europe forgot about them for hundreds of years, and the history of our own bedrooms begins in the Dark Ages.

Beds in the Beginning

The bedroom was preceded by the bedchamber, which was preceded by the chamber (Great or otherwise), which was preceded by the bower, which alternated, in most households, with a sleeping arrangement so basic as to be a life of perpetual camping.

In the Dark Ages of the Anglo-Saxons, a Lord, his warriors and vassals lived by day in the Great Hall, a huge barn-like room open to the rafters to allow smoke from the central open hearth to drift through a hole in the roof. At night, after carousing at trestle tables with their 'ale-friends', the warriors also slept here, often in a circle, feet to the fire and rolled in their cloaks, or else on makeshift mattresses of sacking stuffed with straw which were thrown down on the benches that ran round the room. Servants, who were to get the raw end of sleeping arrangements for centuries to come, slept in corners or burrowed into the hay with the animals in their stables. The Lord and his Lady retired to a 'bowker' or bower, a wooden hut entirely separate from the Hall. Blankets and sheets were usually of coarse cloth like fustian and hemp. For the extremely well-blessed, however, linen and fine wool could be had, a vast luxury.

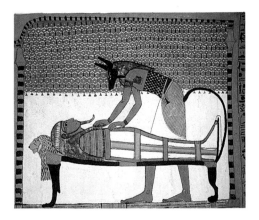

The beds on which the Ancient Egyptians slept – and on which they would eventually be buried – were in the shape of fantastical animals whose naturalistic legs would march them, when the time came, into the after life. The form these beds took is shown by this eccentrically elongated lion with its gently concave base shaped to accommodate the dip of the body, its hard headrest in the form of a mane and its tail providing an elaborate curvilinear footboard.

The development of chimneys in the fourteenth century brought privacy as well as warmth to the better-off members of a household, who now began to sleep in 'chambers', though the word 'bedchamber' is not recorded until 1265 and was not generally used until the sixteenth century. They did not, however, sleep there alone. The medieval habit of bedding down two and more to a bed is one which we find astonishing today. Nor was it confined to the Middle Ages. Children in a Tudor household tended to be parcelled neatly into one bed, even when quite old. The diarist John Aubrey describes Sir Thomas More's famously beautiful trio of daughters of marriageable age as sleeping in a single truckle bed in their father's bedchamber. The truckle or trundle bed was a lowly cot on wheels, which personal servants generally slept on at night at the foot of their master's or mistress's bed. By day it was rolled under the four-poster out of sight. It is generally agreed that the medieval sleeper wore nothing to bed, though some paintings show a thin nightgown and cap. Monks, on the other hand, slept snug. The Bed Laws of Bishop Hugo Gratianopolitanus decreed that they must remove their boots, but keep habits and socks on.

The medieval period saw the elaboration of beds; head- and footboards were carved and counterpanes embroidered. This was the era of the stump-bed, a solid, rectangular affair with, in the better models. a shelf at the head for a candle. One peculiarity of the medieval bed was the number of pillows, so many that they must have slept in an upright position. The chill stone walls of castles were hung with loosely folded arras, or tapestry, to keep out the numbing cold. Interiors were transformed by their rich, glowing colours and scenes of hunting, hawking or biblical stories, every corner alive with verdure, flowers, birds and beasts. This was the first definite move towards decoration in the medieval bedchamber. Apart from the bed, such a chamber would be furnished with nothing more than a joint stool and a chest or two, filled with clothes and linen. These were obviously a practical consideration for a noble family, whose year would be spent moving from one great house to another. You could say that the medievals lived permanently out of a suitcase.

For the poor, living conditions changed little from medieval times until the nineteenth or twentieth century. Most cottages consisted of a single room, open to the rafters like the Great Hall to let out smoke, perhaps with a bower to sleep in behind a head-high screen at one end. The arrival of chimneys in the Tudor period meant that the 'House-Room' or Hall no longer had to be open to the rafters. Ceilings were built for warmth, and provided the benefit of an extra floor under the sloping eaves. Dormers were set into the thatch and a little circular stair or rope ladder led to the 'cock-loft' above. By the seventeenth century this was generally partitioned into bedchambers, each one of which led straight out of the other with no passages, as was the arrangement even in great houses. The poorest labourers, however, continued to sleep in primitive one-storey cottages with beaten earth floors, their animals brought inside for added warmth.

A sixteenth-century stained glass window depicts Tobias and Sarah tucked up in bed under a glorious brocade counterpane, their heads snugly wrapped in nightcaps, a pair of slippers lying awry where they were kicked off. Heavy crimson drapery, hung from the ceiling, shields the sleepers' faces from draughts, and there are supplementary curtains drawn up out of the way in pear-shaped bundles, to be let down when the nights turn colder. The fabrics are sumptuous but furniture is minimal: simple wooden benches stand one at the head and one at the foot of the bed; a single candle stands ready to be re-lit from the glowing embers of the fire to light the dark winter morning.

The Rise of the Bed

The bed began its ascendancy into the realms of ritual in the thirteenth century when it acquired a canopy. Bed curtains had a practical purpose, keeping out the cold and the persistent draughts of ill-heated rooms. But the primary purpose of the canopy, or tester, which overhung the bed was to symbolize rank and power. Originally the prerogative of kings and statesmen, such a canopy was erected over the medieval folding throne or *sella curulis* to indicate the importance of the person who sat in its shade. Chairs were very rare pieces of furniture until the seventeenth century, and they retained throne-like implications – they were used only by the master of the house or a very distinguished guest. In the noble medieval household, a chair would be placed at the foot of the bed in the Great Chamber, which generally gave straight onto the busy central hall. Here, the master of the house received dignitaries and conducted business. It was logical that the ornamental canopy should soon be transferred from the chair to an object with greater potential for magnificence, the bed.

Consequently, testers or circular sparvers appeared above the bedstead. They were not supported by the bed frame, like the later and more familiar four-poster, but were suspended by chains or ropes from the ceiling, and so were more easily transportable. They were simple but impressive affairs at first, completely covered in cloth. Scarlet was the favourite colour for bedhangings, often in worsted, which was extremely warm. By the fourteenth century, the familiar 'four-poster' was taking shape – except that it did not originally have four posts but two footposts and a headboard that stretched up to support the top end of the tester. It was still occasionally carried about; travelling was tricky in those days, and an inn might not have a bed for you at all, or, if it did, it was likely to be verminous. Most people travelled with special 'trussing beds' which could be packed away, but not someone of the stature of Richard III, who, according to the chronicler Roger Twysden, sent some of his retinue on ahead to assemble his favourite four-poster at The Blue Boar in Leicester on the eve of the Battle of Bosworth. He slept in it that night – his last, for he was killed in the battle and the age of the Tudors was ushered in with Henry VII. The bed remained in the best bedchamber of The Blue Boar for a hundred years, a great attraction in its day. Visitors to the inn never realized that they were lying on something far more exciting than Richard III's bed, something only discovered by the landlady in the reign of Elizabeth I, who, on shaking out the featherbed, noticed a gold coin roll across the floor. She guessed the truth and attacked the base of the bed. It had a false bottom which was completely stuffed with solid gold coins. What could be more secure than sleeping on your treasury at night?

But the demise of Richard III and his treasure-bed heralds the golden age of the bedchamber in the sixteenth and seventeenth centuries, when beds were themselves great treasures of resplendent glory.

ABOVE The elaborate canopy of the State Bed derived from that of an earlier symbol of rank, the chair. The Great Throne in the Long Gallery of Hardwick Hall shows its magisterial implications to the full. Indeed it was so exclusive a symbol of power that while a king dined seated on a chair, his queen might find herself perched on a stool.

RIGHT A view into the State Bed at Calke Abbey shows the exquisitely embroidered fabric inside the canopy. Such beds were unbelievably costly affairs, hung with the richest fabrics, even embroidered with real gold and silver thread. The very grandest beds could have as many as eight mattresses – Princess and the Pea-style – topped with a couple of luxurious feather-beds for extra warmth and softness. A plump bed spelt status.

The Heroic Age of the Bedchamber

Before looking at these sumptuous and magisterial beds, it is important to have some idea of the preposterous sums of money they cost. Textiles, until Sir Richard Arkwright invented mechanized spinning in the eighteenth century, were one of the most extravagant luxuries. We may think silk velvet and brocade expensive now, but they were much more expensive then. Consequently, apart from the Elizabethan period when the structure of the bed was richly decorated as well, textiles were the means by which beds gained their splendour, making them potent icons of wealth and privilege. In a great house, the State Bed, as it came to be known in the seventeenth century, could cost as much as the rest of the furniture put together. Even at the lowest end of the scale, fabrics were equally expensive in relation to other household items. An inventory taken on the death of Andrew Smythe, a farmer, in 1557 valued his seven acres with standing winter corn at £2 6s, while his '8 pere of sheets', a prodigious number that reveals him to be quite well off, are valued at 12s, more than a quarter of his land and grain assets. This is for mere sheets. A hundred years later, in 1651, Charles I's bed of 'green embroidered satin' was valued at £1,000, his Raphael cartoons at only £300.

What did these State Beds look like? They were often ostentatiously large. For his wedding to Isabella of Portugal, Philip the Good had a bridal chamber built with a gigantic bed eighteen feet long and twelve feet wide. Until the middle of the seventeenth century, beds were fairly simple in construction, although often exuberantly carved. But this simplicity was balanced by their decoration: flat valances were heavily fringed and garnished with gadroon, a kind of gold or silver braid; hangings were made from silk damask and brocade, heavy silk velvet either stamped or figured, tapestries, deep-dyed wool worsted close-covered with needlepoint, exquisite embroideries and crewelwork. A bed made for Beatrice d'Este in 1490 on the birth of her son was a bold combination of crimson, mulberry and gold. It was the sheer density of decoration and vivid colours which gave these beds their pomp.

The rooms these beds graced were, in the sixteenth century especially, extremely bare of furniture, though rich in colour and texture. In 1580 the King's Chamber at Arundel Castle – hardly the meanest room in the house – was described as containing a bed, a table, and the all-important great chair. Second in importance only to the bed were the hangings on the walls. These might have been of the fabrics used for the bed hangings, but tapestries or gilded and stamped leather were also used. An Elizabethan chamber often had elaborately carved panelling instead, painted in bright, refulgent colours with a plasterwork ceiling above. Light filtered into these jewel-coloured rooms through small panes of glass often painted with heraldic devices and casting a play of tinted lights over the already fulsome colours. The effect was of a rich mosaic of fabulous patterns and scenes, piled one against the other.

The King's Bedchamber at Arundel Castle. Well into the eighteenth century the State Bedchamber was the most important room in the house. The idea was taken to its apogee by Louis XIV, and life at Versailles revolved around the Sun King's levée and couchée. Only the most favoured courtiers were allowed near, and an elaborate enfilade of rooms approaching the bedchamber calibrated the importance of his visitors. Royalty and nobility all over Europe were quick to adopt this arrogant plan.

The Humbler Bedroom

How did the ordinary bedchamber compare with all this splendour? In an inventory done at Lambeth Palace in 1558, 'Richard of the Larder's Chamber' consists of: 'A pallet of straw. A mattress. A featherbed with a bolster. A pair of sheets. A coverlet of tapestry. A little board with trestles.' He has no wall hangings, proof that he is very poor (the less well-to-do hung painted cloth where they could not afford tapestry). But he does have a mattress – though no blanket, and no other furniture at all except a little table. Clearly he favours comfort above all. Humble cottages had no windows or 'wind-eyes', simply drop-shutters of plaited osiers that let in little light and kept out little cold. A village worthy, on the other hand, would have had his bedchamber lit by panes of old-fashioned, thin-polished horn or oiled paper or linen. These must have admitted a dim light.

The lot of town folk was steadily improving, however, and by Elizabeth I's reign, the 'best bed' in many farmhouses was a comfortable and unpretentious four-poster, like that left by William Shakespeare to his wife, Anne Hathaway.

The Seventeenth-Century Bedroom

As in the sixteenth century, a nightgown was worn to bed. Women wore the linen smocks or chemises that were part of their underclothes, while men wore night-shirts of linen. Both were often embroidered. The head alone protruded above the warmth of the blankets and had to be protected by a night-cap of linen and lace, or quilted for serious warmth. Dressing-gowns were sensuous wraps of brocade or velvet trimmed with fur.

Heating and lighting from the sixteenth century until the latter part of the eighteenth century changed little. Most bedchambers had a fireplace by the seventeenth century, but if this provided insufficient heat, a little brazier full of smouldering charcoals was brought in to supplement it. Elizabethans burned pine cones to sweeten the scent of the room. Footstools filled with charcoal warmed icy feet and small braziers were placed on dressing-tables for heating curling-tongs. Sheets quickly became damp and were always being aired: great copper warming pans were also thrust into beds, filled with glowing charcoals which sometimes scorched the linen.

The seventeenth century saw the introduction of more furniture into the bedchamber. Chairs stood ranged against the walls in a row, while the bed continued to project arrogantly into the middle of the room. Dressing-tables appeared in about 1650, covered with a table carpet over which a 'toilette' of linen was thrown. Various mirrors, boxes, trinkets and a ewer and basin were arranged on top. Cushions with fat tassels softened chairs.

While the lives of the kings of France were stylized into a public display, the poor, too, lived very much in the public eye. The impecunious subject of Hogarth's The Distressed Poet *sleeps in one corner of a crowded attic living room, the only small degree of privacy afforded by the meagre curtain running down one side of the bed. We may admire the honey-toned cosiness of the irregular little room with its quaint leaded window, but this is not at all the impression that Hogarth intended.*

After the heavily carved posts and foot- and headboards of the Elizabethan age, the bed gradually assumed its classic seventeenth-century shape of a basic box, completely cloaked with cloth, each corner topped with a finial which was sometimes decorated with plumes. Narrow curtains or bonegraces excluded draughts from the corners, or otherwise curtains were fastened over the bedposts with ribbons.

The bedchamber was occupied as a living room as much as a bedroom. Rooms were less strictly separated by function than in the eighteenth century that followed – a trait that has remained to this day. There were bedchambers where friends were entertained, especially at the morning *levée*, and where women sewed and chattered together; and there were reception rooms, especially on the Continent, which had a bed tucked into the corner with curtains drawn around it by day like a shuttered stage. One reception room still gave onto another, usually without intervening passages, and the bedchamber might give straight onto the parlour or the hall.

In the latter half of the seventeenth century, two developments greatly affected the decoration of bedchambers. The first was the introduction of sash windows with their bigger panes of glass, first seen in Paris in the 1640s. A window curtain was little more than a sunshade until then, and shutters were still generally used. But at this point, curtains divided, bringing symmetrical decoration to windows. By the 1790s, pull-up 'festoon' curtains with decorative wooden pelmets had become more fashionable.

A French painting dating from the very end of the seventeenth century shows the fashionable new en suite *decorative scheme, with the rich red velvet and gold fringing of the bed hangings being used also for the tall-backed chairs and for the table carpet. Ostrich feathers were an expensive exoticism that would adorn the corner finials of the tall, box-like beds in costly bunches. Hangings still bedecked the walls, often in panels made to fit the room, while pictures and canted mirrors were nailed straight through tapestries with little regard for what they might be obscuring.*

16

The other key influence was the work of Daniel Marot, architect to William of Orange. He introduced beds of a less formal, more ostentatious outline with elaborately carved Baroque cornices which flung out gracefully scrolling wooden wings at each corner. They were also exaggeratedly tall (the Earl of Leicester had a bed, probably designed by Marot, which was fifteen feet high). Valances, instead of being flat, were now lavishly decked with festoons and furbelows, tassels and ribbons, the forerunners of the eighteenth-century style. Marot also crystallized the idea of decorating a room *en suite*. Occasionally, chairs and stools had been upholstered to match the bed, but Marot now took this to extraordinary lengths, carrying the festooned valance of the bed right round the cornice of a room and across the window, with bed, wall hangings and upholstery all matching. The bedchamber began to show the controlling hand of a master decorator in place of the patchwork richness that had prevailed.

Novelty and Whimsy

The eighteenth century was essentially a whimsical, feminine, less formal age, and its influence was felt nowhere more strongly than in the bedchamber.

The roots of the new style lay in France. The decoration of the bedchamber was now effected by fabrics, upholstery and later wallpaper as much as by the architectural shell of the room. Thus the whole decorative scheme could be changed easily and dramatically – and it often was. This was the age of swags, bows, ribbons, garlands and puffs of silk as well as of fads and fashions like Rococo bedchambers of porcelain and chinoiserie.

Drapery was no longer a primarily functional element in the enormous variety of new schemes for beds and bedchambers that appeared in the eighteenth century. Indeed some curtain arrangements – such as those of this French design – did not even close. The new fashion was to have the bed elegantly framed in a wall niche, well out of the way of the informal entertaining that was now popularly conducted in the boudoir. Decoration moved away from the stately and the magnificent towards the lightness and charm of chintzes, cottons, silks and satins; walls were decorated with paper painted with delicate floral or chinoiserie designs or with scenes of Cathay, while panelling was embellished with fine low relief ornament that was picked out in white and gold, pale blue or pink.

17

Furniture designed specifically for the bedchamber appeared for the first time, though bed-steps were used in the seventeenth century. Now there were night-tables, forerunners of our bedside tables, with a compartment for concealing the chamberpot; there were washstands and dainty basin stands and dressing-tables frothy with lace.

Towards the end of the century, bedchambers moved upstairs away from the *piano nobile*, which was still the grand floor where public receptions were held. By the beginning of the nineteenth century, the bedroom, isolated from the activities downstairs, had become an intensely private place.

The Victorians and After

This was the age of revival par excellence: Gothic bedrooms, neo-Renaissance bedrooms, pseudo-Baroque and Rococo. But in the midst of the melange, the Victorians were also forging a style distinctively their own. As Lady Baker put it in *The Bedroom and the Boudoir* of 1878, 'Litter is a powerful weapon in the hands of a person who knows how to make a room comfortable.' Decorative litter sums up the look of the mid-Victorian room. Drawing-rooms bore the brunt of ornament, but the *bedroom* – as it now became after centuries of being a *bedchamber* – was a private retreat and therefore filled with personal memorabilia. Its atmosphere was cosy and intimate. The daybed, around which conversation had circled in the eighteenth-century closet, now became a chaise longue and stood at the foot of the bed. Ella Rodman Church in her contemporary decoration book called this 'a necessity' and also advocated 'a low easy chair . . . in which one can lounge in a wrapper and unbound hair before the fire'. This was probably the slipper chair, that comfortable, cocooning Victorian bedroom seat with its buttoned back and box-pleated skirt. In addition, a washstand stood in every room with a ewer and basin, a chest of drawers, a wardrobe, and a dressing-table with perhaps a lace runner. Screens were much used both decoratively and to divide a room. Fitted carpets were overlaid with hearth rugs and bedside rugs, potted plants stood in *jardinières*, and pictures and prints were close-hung on walls covered with wallpaper that was either deeply coloured and densely patterned or else scattered with light sprigs.

Half-tester beds called Arabian bedsteads, of great girth and ponderous solidity, were swathed in a lugubrious passion of drapery, often dark velvets covered with braid as thick as thatch and swaying with gigantic golden tassels. These were gradually replaced by spartan 'Health Beds' of brass and cast iron, shorn of suffocating drapery and sporting spring mattresses. These new inventions were welcomed as a blow to the bed bug as much as for their added comfort and suppleness over the time-honoured sack of feathers.

By the mid nineteenth century the bedroom was beginning to fill up with the clutter so essential to high Victorian style: clocks, lamps, mirrors and sets of brushes and bottles appeared on mantelpieces and dressing-tables, while more and more furniture crowded into the room alongside the essential half-tester bed and chaise longue, and dense patterns vied for attention on every surface.

By the end of the century congenial clutter, too, went out of fashion along with strong, dark colours of the Victorian bedroom. Carl Larsson became the great popularizer of those white, bright bedrooms with simply hung cotton curtains that epitomized Scandinavian design. Rustic simplicity, promoted by the Arts and Crafts movement, vied with the sophisticated cool white fitments of the Glasgow School, and later the colour schemes of the modernists – stark, defiant statements of white and black, with spots of shiny colour. A repeated emphasis on the functional later contrasted with the swing towards glamour that took off in the thirties. Voluptuous Art Deco bedrooms in black and pink, with extravagant use of fur, mirrors and boldly curvaceous headboards, became part of the Hollywood fantasy world which then took the style even further into satin-covered escapism on the screen. On a more realistic note, the simple cheerful look of a typical thirties-style bedroom emerged with its somewhat rustic wooden bed, light and pretty wallpaper, unpretentious furniture and few decorative objects. It was a fairly spartan, suburban style, which set the general trend of the average twentieth-century bedroom. By the sixties and seventies the bedroom had fallen from grace in every way. It was certainly no longer the grand and glittering reception room of the seventeenth and eighteenth centuries, nor yet was it the private enclave of the Victorians, a place to curl up by the fire and muse, or write letters. It was simply a place to go to sleep fast.

Luckily, this hapless phase is being supplanted by a new idiom. What we are witnessing now is a renaissance of decoration and all the vitality and spirit that this implies. Colour, pattern, texture, trimmings, characterful furniture and beautiful beds are again coming into their own. Interiors are becoming interesting again, and bedrooms are drawing on all the richness of the past for inspiration. It is an exciting moment for interior decoration, the turning of the tide, with a plethora of ideas to kindle the imagination, as the following chapters show.

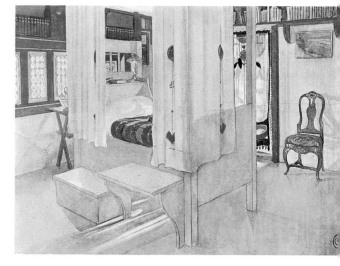

A bedroom in Carl Larsson's own house is flooded with light and decorated in bright colours and bold patterns. The furniture is a happy blend of the Swedish vernacular, international Arts and Crafts style and relics – such as the chair – of a more ornate past. The result is a gentle modernism, and a timely antedote to Victorian excess.

DRESSING UP
THE BED

*After my armchair, marching in a northerly direction,
we come to my bed, which is placed at the end of the
room, and produces a most agreeable perspective; the
first rays of morning sunshine come to play in its
curtains. I see them, on fine summer days, advancing
along the white wall as the sun gradually rises . . .
they are projected upon my bed . . . spreading around
reflections of charming tints . . . I confess that I like to
enjoy these sweet moments . . . Is there a theatre which
stimulates the imagination more, or which brings
forth more tender ideas than this piece of furniture . . .?*
Xavier de Maistre, *Voyage Autour de ma Chambre*

A bedhead can become the focus of attention when decorated with a little imagination. A wrought-iron balustrade gives the bed elegant definition, while a simple swathe of fabric, trimmed with a lace edging and suspended from three projecting brackets attached to the wall, softens the overall effect. A painting can be hung within this framework as a final finishing touch.

The bed should be the focal point of any bedroom, gloriously decorative, immensely inviting. It is probably the largest piece of furniture you own, and the most adaptable. At its most basic, a mattress on a bed base, it is a remarkably unprepossessing object, but such a bed is full of potential. For a complete transformation, little is needed other than fabrics. These are the key to a beautiful bed, for more than any piece of furniture the bed deserves to be dressed up. With the renewed interest in the sheer delight of decoration, the pleasures to be found in fabric, in patterns, textures and colours, this is the ideal moment to put the wealth of new decorative ideas into practice.

Even the most basic divan can become something more than simply a place to sleep when decorated with bedheads, canopies, one of the many different kinds of bedcovers, and a profusion of luxurious pillows.

Bedheads

The simplest way to decorate a bed is to give it a bedhead. Casting the nets
wide, we can take this to mean anything placed at the top of the bed in such a
way that it enhances the bed, rather than simply decorating the wall. This will
instantly give the bed a vertical as well as a horizontal perspective and so
improve its sense of proportion. But it can also be pure decoration, a chance to
be inventive.

An antique bed may already have an appealing headboard, with delicately
carved or painted decoration. Antique shops or auctions are a good source. The
kind you choose will depend on the style of the bedroom, although serendipity
is not to be scorned. If you have such an heirloom for a bed, why not decorate
the room around it?

Many of us, however, have a basic divan to which we want to give a decorative
edge. This is where inventiveness really takes off. Many unlikely objects can be
commandeered as bedheads to bring character to a divan bed: a Baroque
mirror, a coromandel screen, a huge unfolded fan like a peacock's tail, a
feathery wrought-iron gate. Architectural fragments provide rich pickings; a
balustrade or pediment could be used, or perhaps a Gothic doorcase in which
the door-space is filled with padding backed onto board and covered with a
length of fabric.

Comfort also has to be considered. A wonderfully aesthetic bedhead might be
less than restful, but there are two solutions. *Objets trouvés* bedheads can be
made comfortable; a fire surround, for example, can be given a padded and
fabric-covered centre. Padded bedheads look luxuriously plump if well made,
perhaps covered to match an eiderdown or, if there is a canopy above, to match
the headcloth behind the headboard. Alternatively, you can overcome all
opposition to art for art's sake with a wealth of cushions and pillows –
immensely comfortable *and* decorative.

Hanging a large painting or a collection of prints on the wall directly above a
bed can have the same enhancing effect. Even placing the bed under a window,
especially if it frames a beautiful view, can look effective, and the curtains then
frame the bed as well as the window. Positioning is important. A bed that
stands between two sets of Gothic windows will look more dramatic than
between bare walls. And it need not be a collection of prints that you hang
above the bed. A Persian rug, an antique patchwork quilt hung from cloth tabs,
a collection of bright, round Delft plates hung in a pyramid above a plain
wooden bedhead, the choice is endless. Once you hang a large oil painting
flanked by two smaller ones, or perhaps twin bedside lamps, and link the
three with a drape of chintz or voile, your bedhead is well on the way to
becoming a canopy.

*ABOVE An antique quilt, pinned to the
wall behind the bed, can make a very
decorative bedhead. Bold, geometric
patterns enhance a modern bedroom while
the country motifs of folk art traditions
create a country air.*

*BELOW A plumply padded bedhead
represents the ultimate in comfort, either
quilted, deeply buttoned or simply tacked
to the headboard with brass pins, camou-
flaged by an edging of coloured gimp.*

Canopies and Curtains

From a full-blown four-poster to a gossamer drape of lace or muslin, canopies are fast becoming the most inventive and possibly the most impressive way of dressing a bed. They can be extravagant, lavish concoctions or something as impromptu as a spritz of lawn or an embroidered tablecloth above a bed; and though they turn any bed into a *tour de force*, they usually require no more than simple sewing skills. There are three main kinds of canopy: those supported by the wing, those framing the entrance to a niche, and those draped from a framework attached to the bed, like a four-poster or *lit à la polonaise*.

Old paintings and prints are a wonderful source of inspiration for canopies. The eighteenth and nineteenth centuries in particular, when the art of drapery reached its peak, are a mine of ideas. But is is often difficult to see how these sometimes elaborate and skilful hangings can be adapted for a less elaborate age and for rooms with a completely different mood.

A French watercolour of 1883 was the inspiration for a modern-day lit de coin *or corner bed. The earlier design has been slightly simplified in that it uses only one fabric, leaving the interior unlined. This makes it a very simple way of creating a pretty, cosy effect that is particularly suitable for a small room that would not accommodate a grander treatment.*

The key lies in grasping the essence of the effect and simplifying the rest. Sometimes something as simple as substituting light chintz for heavy velvet is enough. Or paring a valance of an excess of cords, fringes, bobbles and tassels or an over-extravagant quota of puffs and flounces. The defining line of a fringe can be replaced by plain contrasting bias binding. Usually it is a case of following just the outline of the hangings, perhaps simplifying the shape or relaxing the curves of the swags for a gentler, less wrought look.

Lit en tombeau

LEFT *A length of striped fabric is hung above a brass bedhead and allowed to fall to a support at the foot of the bed to create a dramatic but simply achieved effect. A cross-braided and tasselled fringe is pinned at the line of the cornice.*

Hang a brass curtain pole against the wall above your bed and you have the basis for any number of hangings: a draped antique shawl or two, a length of silk or chintz thrown in one or two swags over the pole with tails at either side and perhaps a smattering of taffeta bows. Hang a short curtain pole at right angles to the wall and you can invent a plethora of different hangings: a *lit en double tombeau*, perhaps, which translates as 'a bed with a double drape', in which a length of cloth, lined with a complementary print, is simply flung over the pole and allowed to drift out over the corners of the bedhead on either side. Attaching two further short poles, or something ornamental like Victorian tie-backs in the shape of hands or acanthus leaves, below and to either side of the first pole gives more definite swags, the shape of which can be altered depending on the height of the poles.

Put the bed sideways to the wall, and the canopy above now gives it a different perspective and a French Empire feel, especially if the bed is a *lit bateau* (boat-shaped bed), also known as a sleigh bed. The simplest idea of all, perhaps, is to attach a length of lined fabric directly to the wall – this time above the head of the bed – and gather it into a point, pinned with a generous bow. Further inspiration can be sought in the designs of previous centuries.

Lit en double tombeau

ABOVE *An Empire-style bed is surmounted by a short horizontal pole from which a light scalloped fabric is cleverly draped to emphasize its symmetrical form. Again, a stylish effect simply achieved.*

Lit en niche

Canopies are also a marvellous way of making the most of architectural features like niches, or a shallow arch or alcove let into the wall. The French, especially in the eighteenth century, carved deep niches in the centre of one wall and placed a bed or sofa here, the bed with one side to the inner wall. In this way it was grandly framed by the panelling on either side of the niche, and also by festooned curtains adorning the entrance. This arrangement left the rest of the floor space in the room conveniently free. The entrance to the niche provided the ideal framework for hangings of the most sumptuous kind. In the mid-nineteenth century, a lambrequin might have framed the niche. This is a flat, stiff valance of ornate outline, which usually reaches far down on either side, aggrandized with tassels. A shallow alcove can be deepened by projecting a short tester, made of something like chipboard disguised with fabric, from which the valance and curtains are hung. A false alcove can be created in the same way.

A contemporary use of an old idea: French designs of the eighteenth century matched window curtains to bed hangings and even to chair covers for a totally unified look. Here a false alcove has been created by hanging a deep-cut and tasselled lambrequin, or valance, from one side of the room to the other and re-creating the cornice line.

A corona canopy is one draped from a diadem-shaped ornament. Nowadays this can be anything from a gilded crown found in an antique shop to an invisible ring of wire or bamboo hidden within the hangings. A semi-circle of hardboard or chipboard, bracketed to the wall above the bed, is the beginning of a host of possibilities. Cloth can be stapled over it with a valance of box-pleats or swags, beneath which two drapes of fabric fall on either side. A different effect is achieved by hanging a full circle of cloth-covered board, or a flexible wire or rod bent into a ring, from chains or ribbons attached to the ceiling, and then swathed in fabric.

Another clever idea, observed in an English country house, shows how the most prosaic objects can be used to create an effect as sumptuous as a *lit à la polonaise*. A wire basket for hanging plants, turned upside down to act as the basic dome, can be covered in thin wadding to disguise the wire, and finished with a drape of frilled fabric that overhangs its edges. From this, hang four purely decorative 'curtains' to fall in a gentle curve to each corner of the bed.

A feminine variant of the lit à la polonaise, *so popular from the mid-eighteenth century. This simple curved form, topped by a corona, can easily be re-created and hung with curtains, perhaps decorated with ribbons and bows, to achieve the same grand effect without the heaviness of the traditional four-poster.*

Lit à la polonaise

The most familiar kind of canopied bed is the four-poster, a masterpiece of sheer decoration. Only the bed base and mattress are functional, the rest of the structure is pure indulgence. Although the complete effect looks lavish, broken down into their elements you will see how simple they are to put together. Firstly, curtains, in sets of two, four or six, are run on curtain tracks attached to the inside of the frame (they can also be purely decorative); at the top of the bed a headcloth is attached to the frame in place of a curtain; a valance is stitched or stapled above, outside the frame, and another is attached to the bed base below; a canopy or tester forms the 'ceiling' of the bed. Even if you cannot thread a needle, you can easily attach most of these elements with staples.

The tester over a four-poster bed is a versatile item. There are three main kinds: a sunburst, which is gathered, or, more formally, pleated, into a central rosette (headcloths can be given the same treatment); a flat tester, simply pinned to each side of the frame; or, even simpler, a slightly swagged tester, in which a length of fabric is attached to the frame at the bottom of the bed and allowed to bell out slightly like the top of a tent, before being caught again at the top. If it is long enough, a batten of wood can be nailed over it so that the fabric trails behind the bedhead as a headcloth. In addition, there are four basic kinds of valance: flat or straight, gathered, box-pleated and swagged. A grand variation on the basic swag is a row of swags punctuated with *choux*, so-called because they look like little cabbages or rosettes, from each of which hangs a single box-pleat called a bell or *campane*. Such a valance may end in tails, which are simply long lengths of fabric allowed to fall down at either side, usually lined so that the zigzag they make reveals flashes of contrasting fabric.

You can, of course, approach your four-poster frame in a simpler way. If it is beautiful in its own right, you can leave it bare; if it is a slim brass four-poster, you might want to throw a light canopy of filigree lace over the top, hung with little white tassels, tendrils of curling silk ribbon and silk nosegays – a supremely romantic confection. You might simply cast a billow of antique damask over the frame, changing the arrangement of the fabric as often as you like. You might hang curtains without valance or tester; even fringed Highland blankets can be hung in this way to create a cosy, masculine look.

This raises the question of fabrics. Chintz, of course, is shown off to its full advantage by a four-poster, and might be lined with sprigged cotton or a stipple pattern in a colour picked out from the chintz. It is just as important to consider the linings of your bed hangings, as this is what you will see when in bed, and the effect outside is also enriched when a second, complementary pattern shows through the outer hangings. Or you might wish to keep the effect very simple, and make a rustic rather than a grand four-poster. Fresh linen, muslin, crisp white cotton, gingham or ticking look particularly good in summer. In winter, faded antique kelims hung as curtains have a rich, heavy feel reminiscent of luxurious tapestry.

frieze

pelmet or valance

bedpost

headboard

footboard

ABOVE A four-poster bed can be a masterpiece of sheer decoration, yet the basic framework is quite simple. Single and double four-poster frames can be fitted round an ordinary divan bed, instantly transforming it.

RIGHT The great state beds, swagged with yards of heavily tasselled fabrics, were once the most glorious examples of the upholsterer's art. The four-poster bed depicted here re-creates many of the same lavish details, down to the choux and swags stitched to the valance. Behind the pillows fabric hangs from a brass pole to form the bedhead.

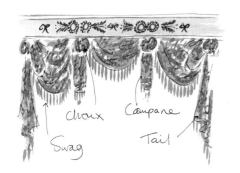

Choux

Campane

Swag

Tail

The four-poster bed

Bedcovers and Bedlinen

Bedlinen is just as important in decorative terms as what goes above or around the bed. The surface of your bed can be used to display a breadth of beautiful fabrics, and interesting effects can be created by combining different patterns on sheets, bedcovers and pillows.

Consider how the look of the bed will be changed depending on which kind of bedcover is used. *Duvets*, also known as Continental quilts or 'doonas', are a big pocket of down and feathers with a changeable cover, and are used without a sheet. They are the easiest beds to make, and have a casual, modern feel. *Comforters*, an American invention, are thinner and therefore neater, and quilted. They overhang the edge of the bed and are often lined in a contrasting fabric. They can be combined with matching valances and pillow cases, and are a good balance between comfort and smartness. *Eiderdowns* are wonderfully old-fashioned quilted covers filled with feathers and down that sit trimly on the top of the bed so that the tucked-in blankets show at the side. They have a homely, country feel. Traditionally used under a large bedspread that is removed at night, eiderdowns can be given a more decorative look with a pretty bedspread tucked in over the blankets and *beneath* the eiderdown. A *bedspread* is any throwover cover, whether lightly quilted or plain, which usually hangs far down if not to the floor. American schemes show an adeptness for dressing beds with a variety of other kinds of covers as well. They use pillow-shams on top of pillow cases so that pillows can be propped on top of a matching comforter, and then removed at night when pillow-cases matching the sheets are revealed. Blanket covers are also used with an eiderdown on top.

One of the most charming and decorative bedspreads is the patchwork quilt. Patchworks are often regarded as purely rustic, the result of a thrifty housewife saving her scraps of cotton and putting them to good use. But if we look back at some of the quilts covering noble beds in the sixteenth century, we see that they are a mosaic of cloth of gold and silver, satins, velvets and brocades which sound very much like patchwork. Cutwork, a quilt of which covered Queen Elizabeth I's bed, can form a similar bed covering, made up of patches arranged into patterns and appliquéd onto a ground fabric.

You can buy patchwork quilts ready-made, of course, and very lovely antique ones are also to be found. But part of the pleasure of the patchwork is making it yourself, something you can do in snippets over months, even years. The patches themselves vary – hexagons or squares are the most usual shapes, but diamonds and triangles can also be used effectively. Some quilts are latticed as well, usually with square patches, in which case a grid of plain cloth edges the patches and also borders the whole quilt as well. Old quilts often had patchwork patterns in the middle of plain quilted bedspreads. A very popular design was a huge star with rings of different colours radiating out from its centre.

Warm and soft, traditional quilted bedspreads are perfect for the smartest of bedrooms, and can be edged with coloured binding to co-ordinate with surrounding bed hangings.

Patchwork quilts exemplify the rustic mixture of the folk art tradition and the practical. They provide a rich and colourful patchwork of colours, prints and patterns in various scales and textures. Floral or geometric patterns, or even a combination of the two, can be used equally well in a rural cottage, a country house or a more modern setting.

Other less usual bedspreads bring a new look to the bed; an old cashmere or paisley shawl tucked in over warm woollen blankets, a faded dhurrie, or simply a hemmed length of pretty fabric. You can quilt any fabric yourself by interlining two sheets of it with wadding and stitching them together in a diamond or medallion pattern. Lace, too makes a blissfully romantic bed covering. The pleasures of starched white linen sheets and ivory-coloured wool blankets, edged with pearl satin ribbon, can be enhanced with lace, either flung loosely over the bed, or tucked over blankets so that they peep through. A lace bedspread tucked neatly in over blankets in this way and then covered with an eiderdown has a lightly layered effect.

Different bedcovers work with different styles. A duvet is the practical, time-saving cover for a city bed. Here, what is a bedroom by night may be a living room by day. In this case, the bed can be transformed into a daybed with the addition of a neat, smart cover that fits over the bedclothes. This will hold them in place and stops the bed looking like a piece of bedroom furniture that has been marooned in a living room. Instead, it becomes a rather novel form of sofa. Piping gives it a sharp, tailored finish, and a piped bolster or cushion at either end will heighten the illusion further, whereas cushions at one end only would suggest a bed. A bedstead with a low foot- and headboard is the most successful kind for this treatment. A country cottage, on the other hand, requires a different kind of bedcover, an eiderdown perhaps. But you can sometimes achieve surprisingly good results with a traditionally inappropriate bedspread if it has the right feel. A patchwork quilt can look right in a grand country house setting, for example, and a faded Indian dhurrie can enhance a cottage bedstead.

Pillows

A profusion of pillows, cushions and bolsters adds a layer of luxury to the bed, and provides further ways of playing with pattern. A varied collection of different sizes and types can look even more inviting than a pile of identical pillows. There are numerous subtle differences. Pillows might be frilled, or have flat borders (also known as flanges), perhaps in a solid colour or white to contrast with the main pattern; they might be piped for tailored smartness, or have a fresh white or patterned border running down one side. French pillows are wonderfully plump and square and look good mixed with rectangular English ones. American schemes are very inventive and generous with big square pillows in large-scale paisley, prints or floral chintzes to which a plain or ruched line of piping is added, or a fat frill. These are mixed with small, round cushions in the same print, piped or frilled, and English pillows in broad stripes with patterned borders that pick up elements of the main print. There are many other ways of playing with different and unexpected patterns on pillows. The bolder and more unexpected the pattern, the more lavish the look.

Bolsters, too, either thrown together with a panoply of pillows or alone, are highly decorative. They can be piped for definition, perhaps in a contrasting colour picked out from their covering print, or else softly gathered in at either end and finished with a fat tassel. They can also be made into cracker shapes or baby-sized bolsters called headrolls or neckrolls, which add yet a different shape.

Mixing cushions covered in everything from matching cotton prints to needlework and tapestry deepens the luxury. Experiment with different fabrics and textures. On an all-white bed, instead of plain cotton use a snowdrift of lace with broderie anglaise pillows and cushions for an irresistibly pretty effect.

A certain formality and restraint is suggested by the tailored look of this array of pillows, piled upon the elegant curves of a wrought-iron daybed. Ticking stripes are co-ordinated with a small, geometric sprig to give a neat, uncluttered look that is accentuated by the flat borders of the pillows and the unadorned bolster.

Pillows can also provide a wonderful opportunity for indulgence: candy-pink stripes edged in soft ruffles and tassels create a very feminine look. An all-white scheme can look equally sumptuous, especially when pillows are given a delicate edging of lace.

ABOVE A soft lavender trim gives gentle definition to the small prints of a country bedroom.

BELOW Alternate rose and moss-green tassels give a bold harlequin effect and a handsome edging to a pretty sprigged blind. Perfect colour co-ordination marries the two styles.

Trimmings

Trimmings can completely change the character of a bed or simply give added definition to the hangings. They can make all the difference between a smart bed and one which looks unfinished. They can also be used to tie in the different fabrics and colours used in a room. For example, if you have a yellow and cream rose chintz on the bed with just a touch of smoke-blue in the leaves of the roses, and smoke-blue carpet and tablecloths, you might run an edging of smoke-blue bias binding along the edges of the bed curtains and hangings to unify the two. On the other hand, the trimming might match the fabric used for the headcloth or the counterpane.

There are any number of trimmings. Even something so seemingly straight-forward as a fringe can be plain, tasselled or bobbled; there are also different designs such as a trellis fringe, or a Gothic fringe, and a different effect is achieved by varying the depth of fringe – deep and generous, or simply a light line of definition. Curtains might be caught back with matching tie-backs, contrasting tie-backs, cord (with or without tassels), or ribbons, perhaps tied in bows. Piping gives a tailored feel, while a frill running along a valance and curtain edge instantly gives the bed a feminine bias. It might be a simple frill, perhaps matched by a frill in the lining fabric, or it might be a mass of Rococo ruffles. An extravagant effect can be produced by frilling tie-backs, the valances, and the bottom and sides of the curtains as well. Sometimes another fabric, perhaps a deep pink pulled out of a pink rose chintz used for the curtains, shadows the chintz ruffles and so gives them more definition. The edges can be pinked, scalloped or cut in points for a deeper degree of decoration and pierced to let spangles of light glimmer through. A garnish of silk rosettes, bows or other ornaments can give a final decorative flourish.

Co-ordination

Co-ordination is an important consideration. You might wish for something as simple as sprigged sheets and pillows for a country bedroom, with the same colour scheme reversed on a quilt. Or you might want to re-create the ambience of the country house by using large-scale prints on the sheets. This gives an altogether richer effect. Many large-scale prints have a small-scale pattern as a background, perhaps a trellis or sprigs, and this is often available on its own as well. A subtle co-ordination can be achieved by using a combination of the two. Borders and linings also make a difference. The counterside of a quilt might match the sheets, or just the border of the sheets. Sprigged sheets might have a striped border for a neat, modern look, or plain sheets could have a border of swagged roses or lace for a more romantic effect. Sheets might match a valance or the curtain lining of a four-poster bed. You can co-ordinate in unexpected ways to give a new nuance to the room. Counterpanes traditionally matched the

ABOVE A bright scarlet trim provides an unexpected but effective and crisp counterpoint to a rose-filled pink bedroom.

RIGHT The same rose-covered fabric can be used to very different effect combined with broad, rose-pink stripes that unite the little bolster, the sheets and the underside of the quilt; swags of pink roses loop their way decoratively along a fabric border at the edge of the sheet, around the necks of the bolster-cases and right round the big square pillows in generous ruffles. Simple silky cord tie-backs at the window curtains and a plain table cloth, both in the same rose-pink, provide just the right degree of respite from the large-scale pattern.

outer curtains of a four-poster bed, but you could reverse this so they match the inner hangings instead. Sheets might match the window curtains, or the edging on a pillow could echo the border to a wall.

The character of a print will suggest how it can be used to give a certain style to the bedroom. Profuse paisleys or rose chintzes suggest themselves for the country house bedroom, fresh stripes or an all-over texture pattern for the modern bedroom and so on. Some prints will give a masculine feel to the bed, especially in certain colours. Broad-striped sheets with a duvet in a tiny geometric sprig will have a crisp tailored look, especially if the colours are navy and sand. Pink and white would naturally create a different mood. Floral prints always seem instantly feminine, and trimmings, too, change the look of a bed.

The final element is that of touch. Your bed must not only look good but feel good to sleep in. Natural fibres 'breathe', and they also have a freshness and sense of luxury which invite you to curl up in them. Their pleasant, wholesome scent is missing from synthetics. Cotton sheets are soft and warm, linen crisp and cool. Pure wool blankets are bliss to nestle into, and the best duvets and eiderdowns are filled with duck down, light as a feather and beautifully warm.

THE RUSTIC BEDROOM

The bedrooms still had their original ... blue-and-white check curtains, the yarn of which had been spun by her grandmother on the spinning wheel lately rescued from the attic ... in the chimney corner, where Laura sat looking up into the square of blue sky ... a flint and tinder box, used for striking lights before matches were in common use, stood on one ledge ... a pair of brass warming-pans hung on the wall ... no longer in use, but piously preserved in their old places.
Flora Thompson, *Larkrise to Candleford*

What is Rustic Style?

As a house, Barton Cottage, though small, was comfortable and compact; but as a cottage it was defective, for the building was regular, the roof tiled, the window shutters were not painted green, nor were the walls covered with honeysuckles.

Thus Jane Austen, with inimicable irony, deflated her readers' expectations of the pastoral ideal in *Sense and Sensibility*. Astonishingly, our expectations of the ideal cottage have changed little since she wrote it, almost two hundred years ago. What other style has remained so constant? We still expect quaint, irregularly-shaped rooms, casement windows, perhaps with lattice panes and green-painted shutters, set deep into wattle and daub or aged stone. And we still expect sprigged or whitewashed bedrooms nestling under the eaves, with dormers peeping out of the thatch and creaking floorboards underfoot.

Nostalgia is the essence of rustic style. It can never go out of fashion because it exists perennially in the past. It does not seek to impress or impose. Instead, it makes a virtue of unsophistication and artlessness, reflecting the simplicity of the country way of life in unpretentious rooms with all the freshness of nature for inspiration. A longing to live close to nature and far from the madding crowd has been expressed by such unexpected individuals as Elizabeth I, who said: 'That milkmaid's lot is better than mine, and her life merrier', and Shakespeare often set his characters sighing for the life of a swain.

The longed-for atmosphere is homely and snug. Flora Thomson summed it up in *Still Glides the Stream*: 'She liked the idea of a nest better than that of a castle, for a castle she had never seen and there were nests in every hedgerow.' A country room should be just such a nest, redolent of warmth and comfort, of roaring fires in winter, a pot of hot chocolate and a candle to read by. There are two sorts of comfort, that which comes with convenience and that which is the result of what Thomas Hardy called 'the human countenance of the cottage', its quirks, oddities and endearing imperfections. The furniture has rough edges, the pictures do not have frames, a jam jar on the mantelpiece serves for a vase. Everything is humble and hand-made, solid and sound. Such comfort has nothing luxurious about it; indeed, it is made all the more delicious by being combined with a certain plainness. The secret to a rustic bedroom lies in this yoking together of comfort and bareness. A rag rug next to the bed gains its appeal from the contrast with the bare, scrubbed boards around it.

At the same time, the rain-washed colours of nature, wild flowers on the wallpaper and the warmth of well-worn wood bring a strong sense of the English countryside into such rooms. Gone are the days when bodgers used to turn legs for tables and chairs in the beech forests of England, but rustic style still preserves the memory of the ritual and tradition of that sort of life.

LEFT Timber beams frame the irregular outlines of the cottage interior. The effect of the stencilling on the walls is light, pretty and handmade, and here the warm, deep pink and green hues are picked out in the patchwork quilt on the bed.

BELOW Whitewashed walls provide a sense of space in a small and sparsely furnished bedroom.

The Classic Rustic Bedroom

ABOVE LEFT and RIGHT Rustic style is happy in small spaces and thus suited to the small bedroom of this shepherd's cottage in Wales. It is a structural style: the bones of the cottage are emphasized, and the pitch of the roof adds character to the room. White paint delineates the skirting boards, door frame, wooden pelmet and the ceiling. Beyond in the hall the ceiling is whitewashed and left bare, but inside the effect is cosier.

The small, delicate pattern of the wallpaper provides light background interest. The central design in sage-green, outlined by a fan shape of cherry-pink dots, defines the colour scheme of the room. Tranquility within the small space is achieved through the harmony of gentle colours.

Co-ordination is carried through to the finest detail: the broad band of pink in the jug, the twin dark green lampshades, and the washstand with its original Victorian coat of paint in fir-green on sage. The furniture is simple, and the crowded effect due rather to the smallness of the room. The bedstead is the classic Victorian brass type, and the green painted hatstand adds an eccentric note and has an obvious functional value. The bedstead, the washstand and the bare-swept wooden floor all echo the familiarity of the comfortable rustic bedroom.

BELOW LEFT A length of starched white cotton, trimmed with lace, is a fitting curtain for a rustic bedroom, framed by a stencilled pattern of curved tendrils in soft green and rose.

Sources of the Style

A servant's attic bedroom of the mid-nineteenth century contains strong elements of the rustic style. Both the comfortable sleigh bed and the painted washstand are fundamental features of such a bedroom. The diamond-patterned rug is juxtaposed against the flower-sprigged wallpaper, a patchwork of different patterns which are yet compatible; and the asymmetrically hung paintings give the room its informality.

The yearning to inhabit an ideal pastoral world goes all the way back to the Romans who invented a special genre of literature to express it. Their Arcadia was an Eden peopled by shepherds, shepherdesses, nymphs and dryads; an ideal antidote to the dusty, jaded streets of Imperial Rome. The most famous pastoral idyll of all was Le Hameau, Marie Antoinette's hamlet at Versailles. Half-timbered buildings like a little manor house, a farmhouse, a dairy and a keeper's cottage were furnished for her in French provincial style. During the Regency in England a version of the fairytale cottage became the vogue, thatched of course, but also sugar-iced with various ornamentations – lacy gables, oriels and bays. The Romantics further popularized the ideal cottage lifestyle, a favourite subject for painters throughout Queen Victoria's reign. The artist craftsman William Morris and his followers saw this rustic vision through rosy medievalized spectacles and designed stout, hand-crafted English

RIGHT The American sources of the rustic style are illustrated by this stencilled bedroom. The oakleaf and floral motifs are inspired by nature, while the strong, geometric designs reflect the Puritan discipline.

BELOW 'Attic', one of Laura Ashley's early rustic prints, was inspired by this tiny scrap of antique wallpaper found in an attic bedroom.

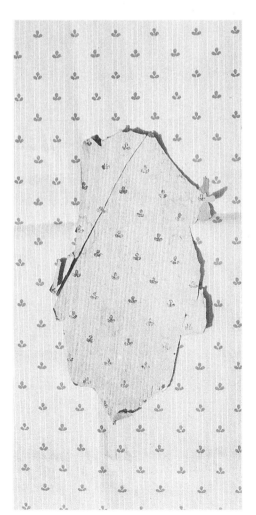

furniture accordingly, stripping Victorian style of its often excessive ornamentation and returning it to the honest simplicity of the English vernacular. The penchant for plain, pleasing but practical furniture was developed further by the Arts and Crafts movement, which carried rustic style into this century where it has remained a widely popular undercurrent beneath the successive waves of glossier fashions.

Servants' bedrooms in many nineteenth- and early twentieth-century country houses display this same attractive vein of rustic simplicity. As far back as 1715, the Duchess of Marlborough could write, when furnishing Blenheim with feather beds, 'I shall want . . . all good and sweet Feathers, even for the servants.' Of course, this may have not have been true, but the first time we become aware of servants having a style of their own and an area of their own in the house is in the well-ordered nineteenth century. They slept in the attic under the eaves as they probably would have done at home, and adopted a clean, spartan style with plain, no-nonsense furniture, brass beds or the simplest wooden ones, perhaps with a little desk for writing at, a basket or slipper chair, a cast-off wardrobe or a clothes press in the corridor outside, a little washstand, a chamberpot, and a rag rug by the bed.

Wallpaper was originally very much the province of the poor, who pasted handbill-sized sheets around their small spare rooms to brighten them up. That was in the fifteenth and sixteenth centuries, and very few examples of wallpaper of the period exist. Many that do are found lining deed boxes and chests rather than walls, and experts are unsure in many cases which of these were also used for walls, as some lining papers were produced for boxes and bindings alone.

Certainly, by the late seventeenth century, small, stylized floral patterns were being printed on calico and other coarse-woven cloths. These were printed with

RIGHT The American version of the rustic style – seen here in the Long Island home of a sea captain – displays the same neatness but rather less sweetness than its English counterpart. The simple blue and stone colour scheme, the traditional federal colours of the early American nation, perfectly play up the mellowness of waxed floorboards and warm sunlight. The Puritan economy of line is matched by an economy of pattern: the small-scale geometric prints, with their rough, hand-printed appearance, are an ideal alternative to the familiar floral sprigs.

BELOW The inspiration for the naïve dotted print 'Sea Spray' was the lining paper of this pretty Victorian trunk.

wooden hand blocks as mechanized printing techniques did not take off until the end of the eighteenth century, and were very probably used as both dress materials and country furnishing fabrics as well as wallpaper.

One typical feature of early nineteenth-century wallpapers is the textural ground pattern, which gives a pinpoint dot effect seen in many cottage sprig patterns, often forming small shapes, or lines. This was the simplest kind of decoration, achieved by sticking brass pins into the copper rollers from which the patterns were printed. In seventeenth- and eighteenth-century America, travelling pedlars took a selection of woodblocks in their packs, cut with pretty floral motifs, and women brought lengths of homespun to them to be printed on the spot. The feathery fine patterns with long, tendrilly stems and leaves owe a great deal to the Indian fabrics which flooded into England in the seventeenth century and influenced so much textile design.

In America, the Presbyterian tradition favoured strong, simple lines and unmannered plainness with subdued colour schemes, traditionally blue and stone, used on everything throughout the period from waistcoat linings to furniture. Terracotta, green and cream was another popular colour scheme, perfectly playing up the mellowness of waxed floorboards and warm sunlight. But perhaps the most important, certainly the most unique, rustic style to come out of America is that of the Shakers. They were a peculiarly American phenomenon, a celibate sect of Puritans who rejected clutter and ornament in life as in furniture. They lived in barn-like, clapboard communal dwelling-houses and slept in dormitories. Their rooms were astonishingly pure, beautiful and empty, totally unlike anything in Europe or America at that period.

Creating a Rustic Bedroom

WALLPAPERS, FABRICS, PAINT AND DECORATIVE DETAILS

The strong lines in the wallpaper design and the curtains of this bedroom create a masculine mood. The simply hung cloth, which forms a curtain in the side window, echoes the log cabin of the pioneer, and the low-backed Windsor chair is a classic piece of rustic furniture.

Laura Ashley recognized the decorative qualities of country prints when she first came upon scraps of early nineteenth-century cotton in antique shops and stalls. It was from these that she took the inspiration for her first furnishing fabric and wallpaper collections, together with the English and French cottage pattern books which abounded at the beginning of the nineteenth century. But there were other, more unusual, sources as well: a nineteenth-century book endpaper, the lining of a battered trunk or an antique music box, and a tiny motif from a stray page of nineteenth-century sheet music.

But nature itself has always been the ultimate inspiration for rustic patterns. Above all, it is native English wild flowers, or those which have been naturalized for centuries, which are the prime source. Cottage sprigs are small and unobtrusive like these wild flowers and have the same discreet prettiness. Their colours are equally gentle; English spring colours of soft rose, moss, harebell blue and buttercup yellow.

Rustic walls come roughcast and whitewashed or dappled with the simplest, freshest floral sprigs. Often, cottage walls are wainscotted to dado height with planks of white-painted wood. These are effective foils for a wallpaper border, which can be used to band the planks top and bottom. The slopes and asymmetries of the cottage ceiling can also be brought out with a border, and the odd placing of doors emphasized by running a border that follows the skirting board up and round the door frame. Borders provide a link between two areas of pattern; if you have nosegays on the bed and sprigs on the wall, a wallpaper border of nosegays will help to unify the room.

Stencils are a very old form of country cottage decoration, an unusual effect for very little expense. They were used in a great variety of ways: as borders, or to cover a wall as completely as wallpaper, along skirting boards, cornices and inside the panels of doors and on furniture.

The use of stencilling to pepper a wall or a border with pattern looks light and pretty and has the pleasing sense of being hand-made which gives an edge to a country bedroom. It can look light and faded or very crisp depending on whether soft or sharp colours are used.

Rustic windows need only the simple treatment given to the rest of the room. Dormers and tiny, deep-set windows with little space between glass and wall will require a curtain on a hinged pole which can be swung across the window by night, back against the wall by day. Elaborate valances are for grander schemes, and white-painted wooden cornices or a simple gathered frill that echoes the

LEFT It is the finishing touches which furnish a bedroom with the quaintness and charm of the rustic ideal. A bunch of dried flowers hung above the mantelpiece and a small posy of fresh flowers in a simple glass jar stress the natural origins of the floral wallpaper. A pair of bellows by the Victorian fireplace and a wooden towel rail evoke the nostalgic mood of the pastoral idyll. A couple of scent bottles create an idiosyncratic note, and a collection of small photographs add a personal touch to the room.

ABOVE The popular and versatile art form of stencilling has a historical tradition from the Ancient Greeks to the American settlers, and is here used to enliven the plain floorboards, the walls, and the panelled door. The green leaf and pink rose stencils are country motifs; moss-green paint is also used on the door. The rush-seated chair is a typical piece of sturdy and simple rustic furniture.

valance of the bed are enough. The low proportions of a room will often demand sill-length curtains rather than full-length ones.

Muslin is the ideal romantic element in a country bedroom. It is extremely versatile and can be draped at a window to shade the sun and give privacy, or else used as the lightest, breeze-catching curtains. It can be stitched into a festoon of gauzy ruffles for a frothy covering on a dressing table or bedside table, gathered along a mantelpiece or draped above a humble wooden bed. Above all, it has the innocence and simplicity that go with a country bedroom.

Ceilings are usually whitewashed, perhaps ribbed with glorious darkened oak beams. Sometimes, however, on sloping eaves, panels of wallpaper can carry the pattern further up.

Bare wooden boards, either scrubbed or unadorned, or bleached for a driftwood effect, have character and pleasing roughness. They can be painted and stencilled too. Rush and coir matting is the natural development from the rushes and sweet herbs Elizabethans strewed on their floors, and their earthy undyed colours blend well with country rooms. Rag rugs and hook rugs are perennial country favourites for the floor.

It is the little things in a room which give it a personal, idiosyncratic touch and bring out the character of the decorative scheme. Dried flowers are a time-honoured tradition, tied with a ribbon and hung upside down on a wall, or filling a basket. Samplers can bring an extra element of texture to the walls, and those of the eighteenth and nineteenth century, often done by children, can be exquisite. Size is important. A tiny mirror in a bigger frame emphasizes the scale of the room, and hanging prints asymmetrically in a group underlines an oddly-shaped one.

Collections based round a theme add interest: Toby jugs, old egg spoons, shells and fossils, old sewing tools, china figurines, crystal and glass scent bottles mingled with old bottles of rose and lavender water, pressed flowers between the pages of a book, old photographs in their frames.

You don't have to live in the country to enjoy the freshness of a country bedroom. Using your imagination, you can adapt a room in a town house to the rustic style; very few people live in houses so grandly proportioned that there is no room appropriate for this kind of treatment, and even then, there will be attics. The extremities of a house are often the best place to create a country bedroom – attics, in particular, with their sloping eaves and low ceilings, dormer windows, and often, smaller rooms. Basements, too, have the lower ceilings more in keeping with the proportions of rustic prints, and they often look out onto a garden or a paved area which can be filled with colourful pots of country flowers.

A dressing-table can be created from the irregular nooks and crannies of a cottage bedroom, or perhaps an unused cupboard. Pleated fabric provides the perfect disguise for less than perfect walls. A skirted table and frilled cushion complete the effect.

The Rustic Bed

The classic rustic bed is either the simple wooden bedstead or the Victorian brass and iron bed, whether polished to a gleam or given a coat of white paint. The restrained elegance of its curlicues have just the right sort of spindly grace for a country bedroom. A wooden bed was the earliest cottage sleeping place, a simple chest-shaped bed with a mattress tucked in, and scrubbed pine box beds and sleigh beds are a development of this. The truckle or trundle bed, which is basically the same structure on wheels, was kept under the four-poster in more well-to-do houses and wheeled out at night for a servant to sleep on.

Four-posters, however, were not the confine of the rich alone. By the seventeenth century, the four-poster was often the best bed in a country farmhouse, and Shakespeare's famous 'second-best bed', bequeathed to Anne Hathaway, stands today in her cottage near Stratford-on-Avon.

Country beds were often in the kitchen through lack of space and warmth. The settle served as a fireside seat by day and the base pulled out like a drawer at night to reveal mattress and blankets.

Well into this century, many Scottish cottages had cupboard beds in the kitchen, with sliding panels or thick curtains to enclose sleepers at night, a legacy, like so many Scottish things, of the French.

The rustic bed need not be too humble to take a canopy, and quite grand ideas can be adapted to a simpler form and different materials. A gilded boss becomes a plain pine one, and a velvet swag, a simpler version in muslin or sprigged cotton. In this way, the plainest rustic bed can be dressed up very prettily.

Furniture for a Rustic Bedroom

Country furniture is a patchwork of styles and periods, the legacy of the cottager who would put together a home from whatever sources were available to him. But there are certain styles and pieces of furniture characteristic of the country: rush-seated chairs and old oak chests, spindle- and ladder-backed chairs, Bible boxes and the old style of armchair known as country grandfather, or maybe a Windsor chair. It was from the Windsor chair on which mothers sat to nurse their babies that rocking chairs, originally known as nurse chairs or Boston rockers, were developed in America.

Other types of furniture also lend themselves well to country bedrooms, especially Victorian pieces which still stand in many farmhouses and cottages, and epitomize rustic style. Few country bedrooms will be without a Victorian washstand, with its porcelain jug and basin.

Swedish Gustavian furniture is extremely pretty, simply-shaped, and decorated with pale coats of dove-grey, duck-egg blue or grey-green paint. Country Georgian was the furniture of farms, small manors, parsonages and houses in country towns, and it is from this period that country furniture developed as a style in its own right.

The country dressing table is usually small in size, perhaps painted or of scrubbed pine with a lace runner or cloth cover of unassuming sprigged cotton or muslin. A small mirror might hang above an attic bed, flanked by bunches of dried cornflowers and daisies.

In many cottage bedrooms, the wardrobe is too big to squeeze into the room. It can be happily accommodated on the landing, which is where the nineteenth-century cottager often kept it. Pine wardrobes, sometimes with a deep drawer at the bottom, can be found in country antique shops. On the Continent, in particular, peasant wardrobes and clothes' presses were often gaily painted or primitively carved, and these are very decorative. Perhaps the most characteristic country solution to storing clothes, however, is to fit a sprigged curtain in front of a shallow recess – simple and inexpensive.

The fashion for painted furniture was inspired by Sheraton's 'fancy' chair in the early nineteenth century, designed to refine humble pine for use in attic bedrooms. Popular colours were muted milky greens, blues and browns. The antique rocking horse and the 1840s Boston rocker with its frilled cushion add character and wit. The Victorian fireplace is decorated with filmy ferns and dried flowers, and next to this a recess provides hanging space for clothes.

49

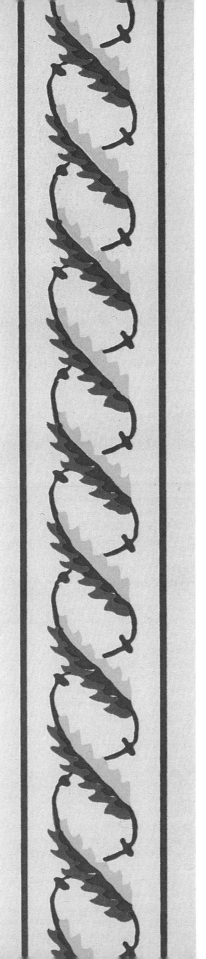

THE
COUNTRY-HOUSE
BEDROOM

*I like the decoration of a room to be well behaved but
free from too many rules; to have a sense of
graciousness; to be mannered yet casual and unself-
conscious; to be comfortable, stimulating, even
provocative, and finally to be nameless of period ...*
John Fowler

What is Country-House Style?

Country-house style is something more than just the grand air of ancient English country seats. In fact, the blend of slippered ease and stateliness we recognize as typically 'country-house' is not ancient at all but very much a product of the last few decades. Yet it *is* a style vividly alive to the decorative possibilities of the past.

The richness of pattern piled on pattern, of flowered chintz next to tapestry rugs, of bold bed hangings next to chequered chairs that characterizes the look grew out of an accumulation of disparate objects in declining houses where once the decoration of a room had been all-embracing. It took the eye of the grand decorators and a new generation of country-house owners from the 1930s onwards to turn plain neglect into a brilliant and immensely covetable style – a style that appears to have taken generations to put together.

One of the tenets of this style is that a room should be comfortable not just to sit or sleep in, but comfortable to the *eye*. It should be sophisticated in an understated way, never overtly luxurious, the juxtaposition of different patterns and styles never strident. Instead, everything is blended and worked together to create an atmosphere of space and harmony.

The secret is perhaps that country-house style does not make the mistake of being too grand. John Fowler, the doyen of country-house decorators, once said that too many grand things in a room made it look 'dead'. Country-house bedrooms wear their spaciousness and fine furniture lightly, nonchalantly. Grand pieces are mingled with simple elements which not only set them off to advantage but bring a human perspective to the room. It was this softening of the formality of awesomely proportioned rooms and the introduction of a note of simplicity which brought country-house style very much into twentieth-century living.

French country-house style, on the other hand, is more formal and altogether a more conscious art. It is less solid and comfortable, more ornate yet less full of possessions. For the French, elegance is discipline and the result of artifice. The English country-house style is born of artifice, too. Asymmetry and mismatching of pattern is used to break up any too formal overtones, but the French do this by taking the room back to its architectural ornament with few pieces of furniture. They like balance and symmetry. The finished look is polished, perfect and taut, whereas the English equivalent introduces a note of imperfection to suggest ease.

American country-house style has always been strongly influenced by the influx of ideas from Europe, with ornate French *fauteuils* and deeply decorative bedrooms lyrical with white and gold – unabashedly *luxe*. In recent years,

ABOVE The elegant, formal architecture of this bedroom from a French château is allowed to speak for itself: the only pattern, a simple broad stripe, is careful not to compete with the exquisite plasterwork, which is picked out in palest almond-green and white. These gentle, demure colours are echoed in the woven carpet that lies on the plain polished floorboards. There is a sense of formality and restraint in this room, yet it is far from staid: there is a whimsical carousel-like look to the candy-pink striped scalloped valance. The country-house look is not about following rules but about having the confidence to follow your own tastes and the stylishness to carry it off.

RIGHT The American country-house style is altogether more flamboyant than its European counterpart, with more than a touch of Hollywood luxury about it. While the English and French imaginations are drawn to faded grandeur and demure elegance, the American style is in a smarter vein, combining elements of European traditions with a sense of extravagance that is entirely its own.

The walls of this American bedroom are painted in a rich, deep baize-green, and the choice of this colour is a bold master-stroke that adds just the right degree of rigour to the plethora of English chintzes. Pattern is piled on pattern and roses abound – in vases as well as on quilts and pillows, carpet and frills – while the elegant line of the four-poster bed and its stark white draperies add a counterpoint of restraint.

however, the English country-house look has overtaken the French as the flagship of gracious living in the American imagination and has been vigorously translated into rooms replete with sofas, four-posters, rugs and pictures. Again, the American love of indulging an idea to the full has led to a daring interpretation with ever bolder and more vivid chintz striking chintz, a fanfare of glorious colour and trunks full of decorative objects. There are few worn chairs and threadbare fabrics in the American version of the style.

On the other hand, in America a distinctively native country-house style has also grown out of the strong puritanical interiors of the northern colonials, and the Greek Revival period at the end of the eighteenth century. In the noble and reserved houses of that period, like Boscabel and Monticello, bedrooms were often much less ostentatious than the rooms downstairs. Rush matting might replace carpets in summer, and cheerful gingham bed hangings alternated with taffeta and silk. A rocking-chair might sit next to Neo-classical pieces by the great American cabinet-maker, Duncan Phyfe. The result, a mixture of down-to-earth puritanism, country simplicity and grand ease, is both fresh and unpretentious.

53

The Classic Country-House Bedroom

The classic country-house bedroom is a room that blends the old and the new, the formal and the homely, the sumptuous and the simple. Here, the bed has been the chief object of the decorator's art, sporting no less than three different fabrics for its sheets, quilt, valance and the glorious heap of bolsters and pillows – yet it does not overpower, as the patterns have been chosen to work together rather than compete.

Elsewhere in the room, a certain sparseness counteracts the plethora of patterns on the bed: the elegance of the room is derived not from lavish furnishings but from the graceful line of the furniture and the classic proportions of the room. The windows are left bare but for simple panels of lace to filter the sunlight with its delicate filigree. Curtains would hide the fine shutters.

Two noteworthy pieces of classic bedroom furniture are seen here: beyond the bed is an armoire, a particularly pretty French version of the wardrobe, of which the panels of the doors are replaced with pleated fabric for a very soft, elegant effect. Beside the bed another faintly archaic piece of bedroom furniture – a set of bedsteps – is called into play doubling as a breakfast table.

55

Sources of the Style

... the essence of cool, flowery chintz,
elegant unobtrusive rooms that rise in the
mind when we think of country houses ...
          Christopher Hussey

Country-house style, as a conscious evocation of the past that goes hand in glove with the comforts of contemporary life, only really began when country-house living was in decline. By the First World War, the old style of grand country living in England had been almost played out. *Nouveau riche* Victorian industrialists, longing to establish a link with the old money, built country houses in period style and furnished them with a mixture of baronial splendour and overstuffed upholstery. The centre of power had shifted and country houses were becoming an anachronism. It was this very neglect, the effect of faded grandeur, which so attracted certain interior decorators. In fact, the style was born from the decline of the country-house and the rise of the grand interior decorator. It was a new way of using the past for the present; a process of shaking up rooms which had become stiff and old-fashioned by bringing a certain simplicity into play with the glorious antique fabrics and furniture. Allied to a profound knowledge of the decorating techniques of the past, this gave these new rooms their authenticity. Middle-class taste also brought something to the style, something less selfconscious and more comfortable, readily adaptable to the bedrooms of rambling rectories, old farmhouses and small manor houses.

Eclecticism has come to be a hallmark of the style, but this is a far from traditional element of country-house decoration. From the second half of the seventeenth century, rooms had been decorated with an eye to unity. As houses were rebuilt in different styles, so rooms were totally redecorated in accordance with the latest aesthetic rules, and old furniture and fabrics were removed. Country-house owners could demand everything bespoke for their houses as fashions changed from the phalanxes of upholsterers and cabinet-makers, designers and decorators, plasterers and painters who prospered, particularly in the eighteenth century.

But in the twentieth century, many of these schemes designed exclusively for particular country-houses were destroyed, damaged or dispersed. This led to leaps forward in the art of restoration, but at the same time country-house owners began to see a new virtue in the catholic taste of rooms which were filled with an array of mismatched furniture and pattern. Decorators turned this to positive advantage, bringing out the character of a carpet or piece of furniture by placing it in new, though sympathetic, surroundings which cut across period and style.

The quintessentially English country-house look was in fact at least partly created by Americans. One important influence on the style was the Virginian-born Nancy Lancaster, a close collaborator with John Fowler. Her own bedroom, decorated in quiet shades of cream and smoke-blue, exemplifies the comfortable, effortless elegance that is the key to the style. No less an arbiter of taste than Cecil Beaton wrote of her 'she has a talent for sprucing up a shabby house and making a grand house less grand ... and [has] brought a welcome touch to many an English house.'

What held these disparate elements together was the backdrop of wallpapers, curtains, carpets and furnishing fabrics. Yet these were the elements which, as they perished easily, had undergone most change. Decorators began to copy carpet, chintz and wallpaper designs they had seen in particular country houses, making these available to an exclusive clientèle, and in this way the fine and lavish patterns of the late eighteenth and nineteenth centuries began to have a broader appeal.

In the 1980s, Laura Ashley started to produce faithful copies of country-house prints, now reaching a far wider public than ever before. Nineteenth-century chintzes, Georgian damasks, Renaissance brocades and French eighteenth-century *toiles*, taken from country houses in England, America and France, were reworked in fabrics and wallpapers, making it possible to express the richness of the past in a way which is entirely of the present.

RIGHT Florence Nightingale's bedroom in Buckinghamshire shows a Victorian application of that favourite country-house fabric – chintz. Linen and cotton bedhangings were much used from the mid-eighteenth century, their coolness and crispness making them particularly popular for summer use, or as inner bed curtains.

BELOW Often regarded as the most English of fabrics, chintz was in fact appropriated from India. The first chintzes – the word comes from the Hindu chitta – began to arrive in England by way of the East India Company from 1600 onwards. When these imports were banned in 1722 to encourage the emerging cotton trade, the flower patterns were taken up by the English calico printers and made wholly their own. This example of glazed roller-printed cotton dates from the early nineteenth century.

Creating a Country-House Bedroom

WALLPAPER, FABRICS, PAINT AND DECORATIVE DETAILS

First impressions of a country-house bedroom are those of colour and pattern: deep greens, rich crimson, patrician blues and lavender-grey, the old rose colours and butter-yellows of sun-mellowed chintzes, the filigree gold and pink of faded tapestry carpets, the crystalline colours on plasterwork, or the dark lustre of thickly-patterned needlework. This strength of colour, in one room, can be surprising, but it is one of the keys to decorating a country-house bedroom and is the source of much of its brilliancy and grandeur.

In England especially, the country-house garden with its ordered riot of clear colour and heady blooms has had an influence indoors – above all, on the design of chintzes. Chintz is the most characteristic English country-house fabric of all, neither too rarefied nor too homely and generally strewn with a profusion of flowers. Chintzes were originally used for bed hangings and curtains as well as for clothes, and in the nineteenth century they also appeared on sofas and chairs. They came glazed and unglazed, but glazed chintz with its inimitable lustre that intensifies the brilliance of colours has always been the most popular.

Other fabrics, too, belong in the country-house bedroom: stamped and cut velvets, brocade and embroidered silks, satin, crimson worsted, closely-patterned needlework and tapestry. Before the mid-eighteenth century, such rich and finely figured cloth was a popular covering for walls as well as the bed, and was used to upholster chairs. Trimmings of gold and silver galloon, deep fringes, fat tassels, and sometimes spangled golden embroideries also garnished the bed. These would be too heavy and formal if applied in such abundance now, but a lighter use of trimmings can subtly increase the sense of richness in a room. Sumptuous antique patterns are now being revived in facsimile on less expensive fabrics: old needlework and tapestry patterns, silk brocades and Georgian damasks are printed on cotton; wonderful Venetian Renaissance prints of gold on crimson, ceanothus blue or Medici green have been stamped on heavy cotton drill with the right weight and feel, specially aged to look like the antique brocades which inspired them.

John Fowler, who liked to throw a note of simplicity against more elaborate decoration, pointed out that linen and cotton could be used with marvellous results in country houses. 'Cotton has been largely ignored in serious decoration,' he said in 1938, 'but many of the English striped cottons and the Provençal flowered ones are delightful. These by no means look "cottagey". Used with a sophisticated background they possess a chic of their own.'

One of the keynotes of country-house style is its breaking up of pattern and colour for a more informal effect. The way in which new prints work with old

These richly gathered curtains are given a formal silhouette with a fabric-covered valance of chinoiserie-patterned chintz in strong colours of crimson and smoke-blue. The opulent carved antique four-poster bed demands that fabrics in this bedroom should possess a certain flamboyance. The strong crimson of the cotton fabric blends well with the deeply polished wood of the bed. Inspiration for the flowered chinoiserie fabric came from an eighteenth-century oriental trellis design.

upholstery and carpets is also important. Colours in reproduction prints have to be carefully pitched between the brightness of the originals and the weathering of years in order to blend well with antique originals and old furniture.

Windows tend to have grand curtains in line with the bed, always full-length. If the windows themselves are striking in shape or elaborately ornamented, they may have shutters or a festoon blind which will not obscure plasterwork or carving, or even no embellishment at all. Something as arresting as continued drapery (the early nineteenth-century saw a fashion for carrying a boldly-drawn valance right over a series of windows) can add bravura in a country-house setting, especially where the bed is also given an impressive treatment. On the other hand, a simple yet elegant feature such as full-length curtains hung inside an arched window without a valance works because of the beauty of the window itself.

Carpets are a wonderful opportunity to add a new element of pattern. The great French and English carpet factories, which arrived in the late seventeenth and eighteenth centuries, produced carpets emblazoned with ornate designs and glowing with colour. These antique carpets – Aubusson, Savonnerie and Wilton – remain amongst the most desirable floor-coverings for a country-house bedroom, their now faded colours mellowing into a mosaic of indeterminate hues. Further richness comes from piling rugs on carpets. On the other hand, the humble and neutral rush-matting used in country-house bedrooms of the seventeenth century, and still used in American country houses today, can provide that element of simplicity which sets off grandeur so well.

The array of eclectic pattern in the country-house bedroom is answered by a catholic taste in decorative objects: photographs in silver frames or collections of china, interspersed with vases of flowers, heaps of beautifully bound books, treen and china boxes for trinkets. Every country-house bedroom can benefit from luxury in details, such as silver- or ivory-topped boxes and silver-backed brushes and hand mirrors on a dressing-table.

Flowers have long been part of country-house life; bringing in fresh flowers from the garden enhances the flowery chintzes indoors. A French bedroom might take a great spray of orchids and foliage in a tall vase, whereas an English room might have several vases of rosebuds looking cool and crisp among dark leaves, or else deliciously pretty bunches of sweetpeas and peonies. Stands, whether tripod or column stands, are the perfect country-house accessory on which to place a vase to give height and importance.

To intensify the comfortable indulgence of a bedroom, cushions and bolsters are used liberally. They also provide a chance to further the mixture of pattern on pattern. Footstools, too, covered in chintz, paisley or needlework, enhance a room's sense of intimacy.

The quietly formal sense of proportion that comes from panelling – both real and illusory – can be enhanced by wallpaper.

RIGHT Sweeping floor-length curtains with lavish use of fabric and trimmings, such as tasselled rope tie-backs, create a grand frame for a sash window. The play of sunlight on fresh floral printed cottons, the scent of flowers, the mellow hue of well-polished furniture and the suggestion of music – these are among the elements that make up the gently civilized atmosphere of a country house.

ABOVE This exquisite decorative plasterwork with its generous ropes of naturalistic fruits and trophies of hunting motifs dates from the late eighteenth century. Country house features such as this should be made the most of; this example has been picked out in shades of green paint.

A country-house bedroom is rarely without its paintings. In English rooms, paintings or little silhouettes are often hung within the headcloth of the bed, above collections of ornaments on a table or above a fireplace, or arranged in an otherwise bare corner to draw it into the warmth of the room. In a French room, mirrors instantly summon the feel of the eighteenth century, especially large pier glasses set into the plasterwork, mirror-backed candle sconces and Rococo mirrors of twisted silver and gold.

ABOVE A four-poster bed need not be a heavy, ponderous affair. Here the solidity of the basic structure is lightened with lengths of antique lace tossed simply over the frame to form a stunningly fresh, delicate canopy.

ABOVE RIGHT The impression of an alcove can be simply created with a pair of curtains drawn back to frame the bedhead. A triangle of slightly deeper coloured wall between the parted curtains suggests depth, while hanging pictures inside the canopy helps centre the attention.

The Country-House Bed

A glorious bed is the *pièce de résistance* of any country-house bedroom. While other elements in the room might be played down, the bed is usually played up and is an impressive though not an over-formal affair. Its provenance is the elaborate and artfully decked beds of the past, but it is not a pastiche of the grand bed of state. Instead, the decorative drapery of the four-poster and the French bed are studied and adapted for a simple, striking look that captures the essence of grandeur while leaving behind any fussiness that would be out of place today.

The four-poster is the definitive English country-house bed, the bastion of every great bedroom; but impressive yet light-hearted effects can be executed with nothing more than a modern bed with a headboard and the all-important lengths of beautiful fabric. The headboard can be covered with cloth, perhaps to match the inner bed hangings or the counterpane, and a half-tester or small flying canopy can be projected from the wall and hung with swags of fabric in a number of ways.

The French, particularly in the eighteenth century, were full of novel and ingenious ideas for dressing up beds. But they also made a number of extremely pretty beds with delicately carved mouldings on head- and footboards which, sympathetically painted to point up the ornament, need very little else to look quite grand enough. French beds were very often placed in alcoves, usually sideways to the wall. A simple but extremely effective arrangement is the creation of a false alcove by hanging a pair of curtains proud of the wall and drawing them back for a pretty draped effect.

Furniture for a Country-House Bedroom

Grand furniture does not make a country-house bedroom. The style is about creating a mood, and too many grand pieces of furniture, particularly in rooms which were not designed for them, work against that, stiffening the atmosphere. Wit, a light hand and a sense of discretion are required. This does not mean that gloriously elaborate Rococo mirrors and girandoles are not a part of the style, but simply that a country-house bedroom must not become a museum inhabited by a curator who reverences each piece of furniture rather than living easily with it.

As eclecticism is very much the order of the day, there are few limits to the furniture you can introduce. While very rustic pieces would look out of place, plain wood and simple lines do not. Certain pieces are typical of the style, however. A daybed or a chaise longue is traditionally placed at the foot of the bed, perhaps a legacy of a time when daybeds in closets were disappearing and the bedroom had to absorb the functions of resting and taking tea by day as well as sleeping by night. This feeling of a private eighteenth-century closet lingers on in the country-house bedroom with its sofas – large, fat and upholstered in sunny chintzes – and the ubiquitous slipper chair. In such a private retreat pursuits such as reading, sewing, painting and simply relaxing can be followed in an air of lofty peacefulness. Writing, too, was often done in the closet, and many country-house bedrooms have a little French *escritoire*, or a bureau, set near the window.

A dressing-table is found in almost every bedroom, but in the country house it often stands under the pier glass between a pair of windows where it can catch most light. Screens are another decorative feature, particularly coromandel or lacquered or else covered with a pretty fabric. They can serve to divide a dressing area or sitting area, but are usually simply arranged to add interest to a corner. Bed steps, too, first introduced in the seventeenth century, are still to be found, now commandeered for holding the odd breakfast cup.

Much of the feel of country-house bedrooms is achieved by the positioning of furniture, orchestrated in a way that is both restful and assured, and at the same time suggestive of simplicity.

A slender four-poster bed is hung with crisp alabaster-coloured curtains that complement its own severity of line with their simplicity. The same fabric is drawn into sunburst pleats to form the roof of the bed. The other pieces of furniture in the room – from the little eighteenth-century walnut writing desk to the coromandel lacquer screen, the flamboyant gilt looking-glass, and the modern Chesterfield sofa – mix different styles and periods in classic country-house manner.

THE ROMANTIC BEDROOM

The best, or, as my wife calls it, the State Bedchamber, is furnished in a manner that has half undone me. The hangings are white satin, with French flowers and artificial moths stuck upon it with gum, and interspersed with ten thousand spangles, beads and shells. The bed stands in an alcove, at the top of which are painted Cupids strewing flowers and sprinkling perfume. This is divided from the room by two twisted pillars adorned with wreaths of flowers and intermixed with shellwork... The chimney piece ... is covered with immense quantities of china of various figures, among which are Tulapoins and Bonzes, and all the religious orders of the East.

William Parrat, writing about his
newly-decorated bedroom in 1753

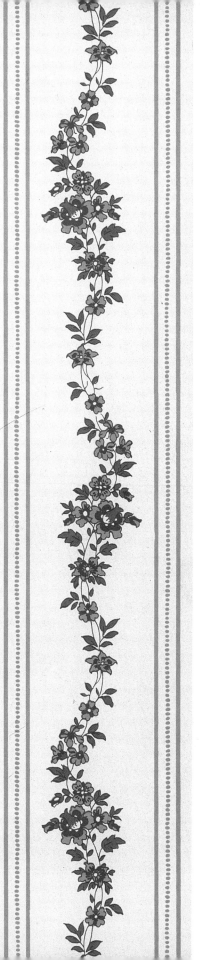

What is Romantic Style?

A modern bedroom takes up the romantic elements of previous generations. Dark, leafy wallpaper creates a late-nineteenth-century atmosphere, while the Gothic curves of the bookcase and the chair recall the taste for all things ecclesiastic that caught the Victorian imagination. Oriental lacquer work imparts a hint of the mysterious East, and counteracts any inclination towards heaviness. Lace is perhaps the most essentially romantic fabric, and this pretty arrangement of panels of lace draped over a plain pole above the bedhead is a simple, effective way of imbuing a bedroom with an air of romantic femininity.

Romantic style is a work of the imagination, an unashamedly escapist style. Function is out, ornament for ornament's sake is in. This is its great attraction – it is a way of expressing a purely personal fantasy that has nothing to do with prevailing fashions or ideas on taste.

It is also the prime point of difference between romantic and classical styles. One romantic room cannot really serve as the model for another in the way a classical room can. Whereas classicism believes in an absolute and perfect room which it strives to emulate, romanticism believes only in private paradises and the capturing of an ephemeral mood or gesture.

The romance of a romantic room is inherent in its inessentials – furniture, for example is carved, gilded, prinked and painted or covered with some marvellous fabric. In this way it gives much more scope for the expression of personality. Here, in the bedroom, which is more personal than any other room in the house, you can indulge your particular romantic dream without having to consider practical questions of cooking, eating or entertaining.

Romance has touched certain periods more than others. Few movements have taken it to more capricious extremes than the Rococo, especially in France. Mr Parrat's wondrous new bedchamber described at the beginning of this chapter perfectly conjures up its colours, its garnishes, its Cupids, shells, flowers and 'ten thousand spangles'; it is a complete whimsical concoction. His bedchamber is sensuous, with jars of scented leaves to smell and the softness of white silk to touch, as well as embellishment at every turn to feast the eyes on. It is a work of artifice and rhetoric and its secret is its indulgence, never one spangle when ten thousand will do.

The East, exerting its eternal fascination from Mr Parrat's mantelpiece, has always been a romantic notion. Cast in an exotic and mysterious role it lends itself to a style which favours the *piquant* and the unknown. Chinoiserie is the more delicate side of this, readily adaptable to the boudoir; whereas the Middle East with its ottomans, cushions, hookah-pipes and rich, intricate carpets and colours, has been the inspiration not just for feminine rooms but for smoking-rooms, studies, and men's dressing rooms and bedrooms as well. The Gothic has also appealed to the masculine romantic sensibility, and has given rise, particularly in its more fanciful eighteenth-century incarnation, to some of the most fantastical bedrooms. It best expresses the dramatic side of the style.

The allure of the Gothic and the East is their distant, unknown quality, their difference from the starkness of the here and now. And this enticing veil of distance in time is also evinced by a gentler, balmy romanticism, that of nostalgia and of flowers. Flowers have long been an element of romantic decoration; their beauty and their associations with femininity have made them natural components of the romantic even in ancient times. And then, what could be more purely ornamental than a rose? They seem like Nature's decoration, purposeless except for prettiness. Partly, too, the romantic character of flowers derives from their very old symbolism, well-understood by country folk, that shades over into the magic and science of the herbal. And flowers were always connected with that other aspect of romance, romantic love, at its most lyrical. Right up until the end of the Victorian age, lovers would send bunches of flowers when wooing from which a message could be read according to the arrangement of flowers.

But there is also a particularly English romantic style that arises from a vision of all nature as a garden, perhaps only possible in such a gentle countryside. Then flowers decorating a bedroom evoke the pastoral idyll of a golden time, never too exactly defined, when people went a-Maying and hung sprays of apple blossom over their doors. Often there is a Victorian feel to rooms decorated in this style because that was the heyday of this very English kind of flowery nostalgia.

Giving the illusion of continual high summer, this flower-drenched room demonstrates the potent romanticism of traditional floral prints.

The Classic Romantic Bedroom

It takes a certain felicitous abandon to concoct a room of such rapturous intensity as this flower-filled bedroom. The effect is achieved quite simply by taking an idea to its limit and using a single print to cover everything: walls, window, bed, tables and chairs are all immersed in a sea of flowers.

LEFT ABOVE and BELOW The print chosen to run riot over the room is of sprays of full-blown dog roses among smoke blue leaves linked with a lattice of star-shaped flowerets and tendrils; the glazed chintz adds its own luxurious soft lustre to the smoky colours. The blue of the pattern is chosen to provide flat relief in the blue carpet and to define edges, picking out frills that would otherwise be lost in the general floweriness. Even the walls are edged in blue, as though they were covered in huge panels of chintz.

RIGHT The bed itself is the lap of luxury, spangled with flowers and frothy with frills and ruffles. It is lined with smoke blue chintz so that the curtains can be drawn for a reflective mood at night and then flung wide in the morning on a world thronging with flowers. The romantic illusion of a room composed entirely of flowers is deliciously underpinned by the fragrance of real ones emanating from the vases of roses and orchids and the bowls of pot-pourri. On the skirted dressing table collections of silver-topped scent bottles, silver-backed hairbrushes, pearl hatpins and fans are all, like the daybed, laden with nostalgia for the refinements of a bygone age of idleness. The whole room, even down to the sentimental pictures in their ornate frames, is the height of full-blown feminine romance.

Sources of the Style

Sources for romantic style are legion, and go back a long way. But while many of the ideas and the motifs that typify romantic style are rooted in the Renaissance, romanticism as a widespread and consciously fantastical style really begins with Versailles.

This palace to end all palaces was originally planned by Louis XIV in 1661 for his young mistress. Although it ended up instead as the most splendid palace in Europe, its light fantastic style owes as much to the decoration of dalliance as to manifestations of power and majesty. Louis's romanticism was that of a Baroque barrage of ornament in an ostentatious vein. But the gilded swags, the built-in looking-glasses, the lustre drop chandeliers and love of ethereal silver were to become the keynotes of the much daintier and smaller-scale Rococo.

This effusively pretty style emerged in the reign of Louis XV in the first quarter of the eighteenth century. The power that had surged in Baroque decoration now melted into the wedding cake elaboration of this most boudoir style of decoration. And in fact the boudoirs and bedrooms of courtesans and demi-mondaines were a fashionable influence on eighteenth-century bedrooms, copied in the very grandest houses. Beds that were once considered quite unsuitable, confections of purely decorative billows and swirls of silk and satin caught up in bows, became the typical French beds of the century.

A dressing table with a fitted drapery skirt epitomizes the romanticism of the French boudoir of the eighteenth century.

The Rococo was above all the style of pure pleasure and of a class devoted to it. It delighted in light, bright furniture, walls often white with silver, gold, set-in mirror glass and such extravagances as ruffles, bows, ribbons a-flutter with flowers, and tinkling glass or gold chandeliers twisted into grotesque shapes. It was best expressed in the fragility and frothy filigree of eighteenth-century porcelain. Whole rooms were encrusted with porcelain swags and flowers like the Porcelain Room at the Palazzo de Capodimonte. The French styles of that century were essentially feminine. Looking back on it, the novelist J.-K. Huysmans (a later, more decadent incarnation of the romantic) wrote:

The eighteenth century is, in fact, the only age which has known how to envelop woman. . . shaping its furniture on the model of her charms. . .

These styles travelled well to England as the description of Mr Parrat's bedchamber shows. But the English love of the whimsical and the quaint was particularly charmed by another fantasy, chinoiserie. This was a genteel daydream of an effete and civilized existence, supposedly lived in the far-off land of China, a place as distant from eighteenth-century England as though it had been on the moon. This, of course, allowed, for its romantic incarnation. Chippendale designed a number of pieces in this elegant, limpid style. It broke all the classical rules that had resurged in England at the beginning of the century and was very much a style based on ornament.

RIGHT *This delightful painted porcelain plaque shows all the sugary charm of a mid-eighteenth-century boudoir. Furniture and woodwork are painted white, and the same candy-pink striped fabric of the bedhangings is used for the chairs in a fashionably* en suite *decorative scheme. The all-white bedclothes are a mass of lace trimmings and frills, pillows and bolsters, quilts and counterpanes, while on the bedhead above, a pair of kissing love birds and a garland of roses are surely the last word in romantic ornament.*

ABOVE *A mid-eighteenth-century wallpaper shows many of the romantic preoccupations of Rococo decoration in its airy design of birds swooping in and out of swags and garlands of roses.*

If chinoiserie and the Rococo were highly feminine, the Gothic taste was a particularly masculine expression of romantic style, epitomized by Walpole and Beckford. Walpole's Gothic interiors at Strawberry Hill showed the typical eighteenth-century lightness of touch missing from the more turgid Gothicism of the Victorians. They dismissed him as 'gimcrack' Gothic, and he himself later admitted that Strawberry Hill was as much the product of his fantastic imagination as period authenticity. He also pioneered the Gothic novel with its drama, its overwrought terrors and wild fantastical scenes, much read at the time by genteel ladies no doubt sitting safely with their feet on a Rococo or chinoiserie footstool in a far different landscape. His Gothicism had something of this escapist relish, as did Beckford's. Beckford was another novelist in an even more phantasmagorical style and a millionaire who built Fonthill Abbey, the melodramatic, Gothic folly with an incredibly tall tower which housed the bedrooms.

Beckford's taste for exoticism had been fostered in his childhood by the fantastic Egyptian Hall of his father's Wiltshire mansion, Fonthill Splendens. He was also interested in the Oriental, not the Chinese, but the Arabian version. The cult of the East influenced decoration not least in the invention of tent rooms. These were first of all a male preserve, associated with the campaign tent and hung with ornamental trophies of war. One of the first was designed in 1777 for the Comte d'Artois. But a few years on, the tented boudoir was the fad amongst fashionable women, who covered the walls with fabric and pleated the ceiling with a tent-like canopy that rose up in the middle. Such rooms were imbued with all the languorous exoticism of the East, their occupants reclining in turban and slippers to take tea with guests.

A return to Nature as a vision of all that was good was heralded by the Romantics in England. The romantic imagination always seeks to charge things with emotional significance, and they saw nature in an intensely romantic light, whether the wildness of the moors or the meditative innocence of a flower. They ushered in an age which worshipped innocence, and looked back to a pre-industrial golden age in which the romantic sweetness of flowers acted as a symbol of both.

The turn to nature in decoration was also reflected in the new importance of gardens. Georgian houses had yards, even in small towns, but Victorian houses, even in the heart of London, *had* to have a garden. Gardening became a romantic middle-class pursuit, particularly the cultivation of flowers, and these drifted naturally indoors, too, in the shape of great bunches of cut flowers which now adorned every room with their fragrance and freshness, and pot plants, which appeared everywhere. The garden was everyone's link with that poetic nature beyond the city. The profusion of flowers spread over chintzes and sprigged cottons, over wallpaper that bloomed with mellow roses twining on trellises, and tangled in the carpets. The appeal of this sunny, pastoral vision has been a potent source of Laura Ashley style from the beginning. 'Happily romanticism is more in the air than ever,' wrote Laura Ashley. 'I bicycle through the London villages, from Chelsea to Hampstead, and the gardens are overflowing with roses and lavender.'

ABOVE LEFT A pagoda-like four-poster, designed by Waring and Gillow in the Chinese Chippendale manner, hints at the romance of the exotic East in this otherwise solid Edwardian bedroom.

ABOVE A bed en niche *in the eighteenth-century French style is screened at night by layers of lace.*

Creating a Romantic Bedroom

WALLPAPER, FABRICS, PAINT AND DECORATIVE DETAILS

Lady Montdore's room, was done up in the taste of her own young days when she was a bride; the walls were panelled in pink silk covered with white lace, the huge wickerwork bed on a dais had curtains of pink shot silk. The furniture was white with fat pink satin upholstery outlined in ribbon roses. Silver flower vases stood on all the tables, and there were many photographs in silver frames.
(*Love in a Cold Climate*, Nancy Mitford)

Lady Montdore's colour scheme is typical of the French eighteenth-century fashion for sugar pink, white and silver, utterly feminine and somewhat fey. It is unusual for a colour scheme to survive intact from another age, but that particular sort of confectionary prettiness has never been better expressed than by this combination of colours, sometimes with the addition of others of the same sweetness – aquamarine, periwinkle blue, a few flashes of gold, or perhaps the deliciously sharp contrast of liquorice black tables and chairs.

Her technique of hanging white lace over pink silk on the walls is equally reminiscent of the French. Not only is it extravagant, but the effect of the pink peeping through the filigree pattern of the lace is the sort of delicate elaboration beloved of the Rococo age. The same flourish characterizes the very pretty eighteenth-century French wallpapers and fabrics. Patterns of fluttering ribbons tied into dainty bows to catch a spray of tiny roses, loops of lacy ribbons wound through flowers in baskets with barley-sugar shells, all have the lightness and caprice that fit this sort of femininity.

The key to decorating a romantic bedroom lies in the matching and emphasizing of patterns, unlike the deliberate mismatching of rustic or country-house style. A romantic bedroom is a sustained effect, it is *tour de force* decorating that must be total to be effective. And when the master pattern is delicate, it must be used abundantly if it is to set the tone. The generous use of a fabric has something romantic in itself, a complete plunging into a particular mood which heightens its drama. So in the Rococo bedroom, in the tent room and classic romantic bedroom the eye is completely arrested and ravished by a single pattern which sweeps the whole room into its idiom and gives one the feeling of having entered a completely different world.

Trompe l'oeil is much used in romantic bedrooms where the idea is to create an illusion. The rippling watered silk effect of moiré wallpaper is the sort of spur to the imagination a romantic room provides. The walls, in an elegant artifice, undulate with ripples that catch and reflect the light. The sense of movement

Details are an important part of any decorative scheme, and can add to the sense of drama and romance. This enormous bow with its long tails and emphatic edging is an extravagant, flamboyant way of hanging a small picture.

this brings, the counterfeit of some ethereal effect as well as simply the imitation of something as voluptuous as silk, and the adoption of a serpentine line, all are highly romantic.

The wonderful advantage of this style is that it relies on fabric, on wallpaper, on paint effects and eye-catching details and not on architectural features. With country-house style for example, panelling, or at least a dado rail, cornice and spacious proportions are an inestimable advantage; with rustic style sloping eaves and dormer windows create atmosphere; and every period in period style has features which make it more easily adapted to one kind of room or another. But romantic style can be created anywhere.

This is partly because it can be so many things. A large and lofty room might take a grand and extravagant romantic style, a small one would respond well to the daintiness of the Rococo, a cottage bedroom or a city attic to the romantic pastoral style and so on. On the other hand, it is even more romantic to turn a city attic into a Rococo boudoir or an exercise in grand romanticism, to throw up a tent room in the country, or a room of rustic simplicity in the lofty space of a country house. Romantic style is about breaking the rules and escaping from restrictions. It is imaginative and responds inventively to the dullest and pokiest of spaces. In fact, the least loved, most awkward or cramped room in the house can often be transformed by the dramatic interpretation of a grand romantic notion, and a fund of wonderful ideas, fabrics and wallpapers are all you need. Romantic style is about mastering the art of illusion and having the spirit to decorate with a total mood in mind.

As a romantic bedroom has an element of fantasy, this is the place to indulge in whimsical objects with a romantic history, and conversation pieces. For those who cannot resist picking up fascinating objets d'art, it is a chance to let their imaginations run away with them. 'I will not attempt to describe it minutely', wrote William Parrat of his wife's Rococo dressing-room, 'it is so full of trinkets.' And in fact the more effervescent romantic bedrooms require a repertoire of bibelots to play up their prettiness. A dressing-table might be covered with a decorative disarray of jewels, powder boxes, little mirrors, fans, china bowls of pot-pourri, silvered scent bottles and crystal and silver vases. Candlesticks, too, look right, and candles generally are a highly romantic way of lighting a room. The pastoral bedroom might have a simple candlestick with a finger-loop for carrying it up to bed. Something as airy and pure as the free-flowing loops of a cast-iron chandelier evokes a different look.

Adding a frill or a ruffle to the edge of a curtain or a cushion, softening the line of a chair with a skirt or a squab cushion, adding a muslin frill to the line of a mantelpiece, these are the sort of finishing touches which give a romantic edge to a room. Pink chintz bows on the dressing table, the frilled effect of the bed taken right down to frilling the tie-backs, make the room convincing, and give it

The floral borders of the fabric thrown over the bedside table, the ruched curtains and the matching bedlinen together with the scattering of pretty objects give a feminine touch to this contemporary bedroom.

ABOVE A ribbon intertwined with roses has been a recurring romantic motif on fabrics for centuries.

ABOVE RIGHT The traditional kidney-shaped dressing table is given a fresh lease of life frilled and skirted with a flowered print in the nineteenth-century manner.

lightness and crispness. Romantic details can lift an otherwise pleasant but unexceptional room. They are props to play with.

Windows, like beds, are a superb opportunity for a piece of pure romance. Simple long chintz curtains billowing in a gentle breeze or caught back with cords or tie-backs can be romantic. Muslin can be used in elaborate ways without seeming ponderous because of the lightness of the fabric, and is particularly attractive in a pastoral romantic bedroom. Lavish ruches and ruffles on festoon blinds, flowered curtains with swagged valances caught with bows and *choux* add essential romance to a headier version of the style.

Ceilings in a romantic bedroom can also be given an air of fantasy. It could be simply the fillip of a muslin or chintz sleeve tied in a bow to disguise the electric wire of a chandelier or a lamp; it could be the painting up of the plaster moulding of a ceiling rose with echoes of the pink and cream used below. Eighteenth-century bedrooms delighted in ceilings of painted clouds. Pale sapphire paint, thinned with white spirit and sponged over deeper sapphire, will give the suggestion of vague cirrus clouds; not too obtrusive.

When everything else in the room is set to lure the eye, plain boards or the unobtrusive, plush surface of a very soft fitted carpet have opposite, but interesting, textures that can subtly enhance the mood in different ways. Beautiful rugs, of course, look as lovely in a romantic bedroom as anywhere else and an Eastern tent room might be furnished with a mosaic of Turkish or Persian carpets. In a pastoral bedroom you can scatter bare boards with sweet herbs as they used to do in sixteenth-century England, so that when you walk across the floor you crush them, releasing the scent.

Some of the most romantic decorative inspiration comes from eighteenth-century France, where the idea of the feminine boudoir reached its apogee. Here the French idea of a day-bed in a niche is given a modern application with this small sofa, framed by a deep-cut lambrequin valance with long side-pieces, bedecked with fringing and hung with generous tassels. The trellis patterns of ribbons and garlands that decorate the curtain fabric and the wallpaper behind were based on French prototypes.

Furniture for a Romantic Bedroom

As romantic style is about freeing the imagination to follow its whims and indulge its desires, there is no limit to the kind of furniture it can embrace. Pieces that are whimsical or downright bizarre are perfectly at home here, and one of the pleasures of such a room is finding the fanciful furniture to fill it. At the same time, solid and unadventurous pieces like an ordinary chest of drawers or a plain wooden chair are easily drawn into the mood, softened with a drift of muslin or a lace runner, and given some interest with a collection of china and photographs. A chair can be quickly dressed up with a squab cushion in a pretty chintz, perhaps to match the bed hangings, and tied on with ribbons and bows.

The lynchpin of many romantic bedrooms, a skirted dressing-table, is created out of the most ordinary materials. A simple rectangle of chipboard, resting on a base, is then decked with a generous skirt of fabric falling to the floor, perhaps with the addition of ruffles and bows and a frill falling over the edge of the table. It can be covered with a flowered chintz or sprigged cotton, or, as it was originally done in the eighteenth century, a crisp concoction of lace and bows. A toilet mirror is set on top, perhaps an antique mirror with a set of drawers for holding powder and trinkets. This transformation of something quite ordinary is like a sort of *trompe*, an imaginative gesture of the kind that the romantic delights in. Covering chipboard tables with floor-length tablecloths in a print to match the wallpaper, or the bed hangings, is another inventive way of adding a more generous feel to a room.

Furniture with a flourish is romantic, even if the flourish is no more than a winsome round cushion with a huge frill that turns it into a scallop shell. The furniture of French eighteenth-century rooms in particular is highly feminine, and dainty. Painted furniture has a soft and often feminine feel to it. A Victorian chest of drawers painted in snuff brown and soft sea green will suit a more reflective, pastoral, romantic bedroom. A Lloyd loom sofa, when painted white, adds its lightness of weight to a more ethereal room.

In general, romantic style is a chance to indulge in decorative pieces and to heighten them further. Any surface decoration – veneering, marquetry, inlay, or the more exuberant gilt mounts – can be played up to the full. It is a playful style that can be almost anything, except prosaic.

The Romantic Bed

The bed is the focus of any romantic bedroom, its showpiece, the key that sets the mood. Even a rain of white muslin, simply framing the bed, is a gesture of romantic decoration. Wonderful effects can be contrived for a bed using fabric

and a little imagination. The most modest bed can also be transformed by the addition of a four-poster frame for more decorative possibilities.

Muslin is consciously innocent, naive. It is a fabric that anyone can afford to be extravagant with. So, too, are the flowered cottons in all their many blossoms and colours. Romantic style can be effected without expensive materials – the secret is to be lavish with them. The more exotic end of the spectrum requires frills and flounces and complementary linings of lightly sprigged or plain coloured fabric to set them off. A *couronne* bed demands drapes that sweep down in long deep folds with an excess of fabric cascading softly to the floor on either side to give that slumbrous, negligent feel.

At the other end of the romantic spectrum are the ottomans of the East. A tent room is perhaps the most romantic bedroom of them all, in which the whole room becomes the canopy and curtains of a *nonpareil* bed, with true romantic excess.

ABOVE The dressing-table, with its fabric skirt trimmed with bows, lends a feminine air with a pitcher of fresh flowers, silver-topped toilette bottles and a delicate Victorian lacquered and gilded chair.

RIGHT An abundance of lace draped over a Victorian brass four-poster and used as a broad border below the cornice, together with festoons of ribbons and garlands of silk flowers give this room its sense of old-world, fairy-tale romance. An early Laura Ashley wallpaper in terracotta and cream provides the muted background to the soft pinks and whites of the room.

THE PERIOD
BEDROOM

Insofar as style is concerned the modern Frenchman dwells in the eighteenth century, he sleeps in that century likewise, but he dines in the sixteenth, then on occasion he smokes his cigar and enjoys his coffee in the Orient, while he takes his bath in Pompeii ...
Jacob von Falke, *Art in the House*, 1873

What is Period Style?

In Proust's *A la Recherche du Temps Perdu* Swann bites into a madeleine and by means of this single *aide-memoire* conjures up his monumental vision of the past. Period style is about finding keys that will unlock the past in this way. Sometimes a single poignant detail, the equivalent of Proust's madeleine, can summon the whole flavour of an era. More often, however, it requires a great deal of thought and artistry.

Period style is, of course, an opportunity to indulge nostalgia, and why not? Period rooms are no longer just for antiquarians and incurable romantics; they are for the most stylish decorators and the most unassuming homes alike. The reproduction of fabrics, wallpapers, borders and other furnishings in every major period from the Elizabethan to the Edwardian and beyond, has made the inspiration of the past accessible to everyone.

There are two ways to use this inspiration. One is to take the elements of different periods and weave them together with a personal idiosyncracy which leads to something entirely new yet redolent of the past. The other approach is to take the character of an era, its fabrics, wallpapers and furniture, as the starting point, an approach that results in a rich sense of period. This is the purer and the more Proustian attitude, an attempt to bring a specific period to life through creative effort.

Yet, even in the re-creation of period rooms, the current age cannot help but add something of itself to the style. The Victorians were great advocates of period decoration, but their interiors always seem to us to be stubbornly Victorian. No doubt the same is true now no matter how sophisticated we may be about it. Our attitude to period style has become less sentimental, more cool and appraising. Knowledge of period interiors has to be combined with a sensitivity for hunting out furniture, pictures and decorative objects which will fit the mood, and above all, with the creative ability to put all these elements together to make a room which not only has the atmosphere of the period but is comfortable to live with. A period must be an inspiration, not a strait jacket, it is not about piecing together museum room-sets. Comfort should not be sacrificed to academic authenticity, and the final test of such rooms is their adaptability to modern life.

The picture essays that follow look closely at successive periods from the Elizabethan to the Edwardian, giving a detailed sense of the decorative ideas of the age and how they can be put into practice. The elusive essence that flows through a particular period can be re-created to make it live again, like Proust's little madeleine.

This classically masculine bedroom re-creates the graceful style of the Regency period with its elegantly restrained curves. Regency tastes favoured strong, clear colours; here a vivid yellow wallpaper printed with a moiré pattern also reflects the vogue for trompe l'oeil *papers printed in imitation of textiles, which reached its peak at this time. The curtains take up the same moiré pattern. A simple fabric border and a gracefully swagged silk rope provide the merest hint of a valance, as well as intimating the maritime preoccupations of the period, also picked up in the rope-and-shell motifs that decorate the dressing-table and looking-glass.*

RIGHT Period re-creations are not a new idea: the Victorians, too, were fond of stylistic revivals. This bedroom scheme was based on a nineteenth-century book of designs expounding the fashionable 'Old French' style of decoration – those styles fashionable at the time of Louis XV and Louis XVI – which included a scheme for a lit en niche. *The pink and grey medallion print used here was, appropriately, taken from an eighteenth-century printed cotton. This has been carried over both the bed and the window walls, unifying the room; the tumbling flounces of the valance with its double frill adds a sense of playfulness, while the delicately striped wallpaper glimpsed between the curtains offers a muted foil to their exuberance.*

BELOW RIGHT Period style is not just for grown-ups – and little boys' rooms need not be brash, high-tech environments. This thirties-style child's bedroom is decorated with racing cars, ships, trains and aeroplanes inspired by the motifs of Boy's Own *annuals. The furniture has a pleasing plainness that is eminently practical. The high bed and Victorian bed steps would delight any child, while the neat, spartan old school desk is there to encourage homework.*

An Elizabethan Bedchamber

LEFT The overall impression of this Elizabethan bedchamber is of dark wood set off by the rich, glowing colours of the bed hangings. But oak darkens with age and smoke, and would once have been a warm chestnut brown, the heavily carved panelling painted with deep, brilliant colours: garnet, royal blue, madder, dragon's blood, verdant green, all shot through with threads of gold.

FAR RIGHT BELOW The bed was the focus of attention, the more richly hung and splendidly carved the better, as the bedchamber of a great house was a formal reception room where guests of rank were received. The hangings were simply arranged for they still had to perform a practical as well as a decorative function by keeping the occupants warm and draught-free at night when the curtains were drawn all round the bed. By day they were drawn up into pouches off the floor. The flat valances at top and bottom were additional draught-excluders and of heavy, warm fabrics that were richly figured and embroidered. The flamestitch design shown here, printed on linen union, echoes the needlework patterns and thick stitches of the period.

RIGHT ABOVE An important detail is the oriel window. Curtains did not make an appearance until the middle of the seventeenth century and the rare glass, stained or painted with heraldic designs, cast a jewel-like light into the room.

RIGHT BELOW Gilded wall hangings might also have decorated the Elizabethan bedchamber.

A Stuart Bedroom

The bedroom depicted here could be that of a prosperous Stuart farmhouse with its long, low proportions, stone-mullioned casement windows, oak beams and seasoned oak floorboards. It is an eclectic compromise, its period details ranging from one end of the seventeenth century to the other.

LEFT The en suite *style of the room, with every element linked by a single major pattern, is reminiscent of the style of Daniel Marot, Minister of Works to William of Orange and who came to Britain with him in 1688. The velvets and inner bed hangings of sprigged satin of the period have here been replaced by a light but elaborate floral pattern with inner bed hangings of sprigged cotton. Wallpaper, borders, bed hangings, counterpane and window curtains all echo the mixture of rosebuds and tangled garlands.*

LEFT AND FAR LEFT ABOVE The bed itself is a composite piece, using Jacobean panelling. By the middle of this period bed frames were no longer decorative but were hidden completely by sumptuous fabrics elaborately garnished with fringes and tassels.

FAR LEFT BELOW Alternatively, an earlier Jacobean mood can be summoned with walls in more subdued colours of navy and sand; the bed is hung with a faux needlework design of stylized acorns and oak leaves.

FAR LEFT CENTRE This Queen Anne dressing-table, with its ivory-handled brushes and silver-topped bottles, heralds the eighteenth century.

85

A Louis XVI Bedroom

LEFT This bedroom perfectly typifies the delicate, refined taste of eighteenth-century France with its floor-length 'French' windows, huge mirrors and vivid colours. By night the lustre-drop chandeliers would have magnified the brilliance of the candles with their rock crystal or glass pendants, the whole effect intensified by the mirror's reflections.

Kingfisher-blue stripes provide the backdrop for the elegant curves of the furniture, above all the bed. Furniture tended to be delicate rather than grand, like the occasional table on its long tapered legs. The bed epitomizes the period, a lit à la polonaise, *set in typical French fashion sideways against the centre of a wall and surmounted by a domed canopy, supported on S-bend iron posts. This is in marked contrast to the flat-topped, box-shaped beds of the sixteenth and seventeenth centuries.*

Silk was the height of sophistication for bed and window drapery. This pattern is taken from an eighteenth-century Lyons silk design and is printed on cotton sateen, whose smooth, satin-like weave gives it a luxurious sheen.

FAR LEFT, TOP Beneath the gilded dome, a little swagged canopy catches up the fabric into occasional choux, *revealing the intricate art of the upholsterer.*

FAR LEFT, BELOW Ornamental sconces or candle brackets are a very decorative form of lighting, instantly evocative of period. Panelling is picked out in kingfisher-blue, reaffirming the framework of the room, an effect that can be easily achieved in the absence of period panelling.

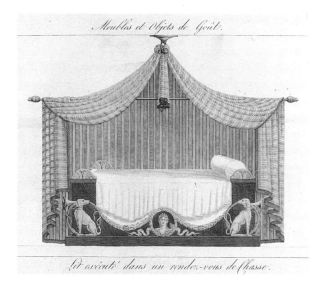

The Empire Bedroom

Empire style began in Paris at about the time of the Revolution, and was born of Napoleon's desire to re-create the grandeur of Imperial Rome and the ancient world. The style spread rapidly across Europe; in England it became known as Regency style after the Prince Regent, the future George IV.

FAR LEFT ABOVE A design of 1804 for a 'hunting bed' shows the spirit of Empire style. Its striped aquamarine hangings, edged with purple, are suspended from a ring fixed to the ceiling and are draped to either side over a brass rod with decorative finials.

LEFT ABOVE The pictures and ornaments on the mantelpiece capture the flavour of the time with their romanticized Classicism – the Empire-style costumes depicted on both reflect the more informal atmosphere that prevailed.

RIGHT This elegant bedroom from a French château picks up the symmetry and grace of the Empire style. Softly draped muslin is used for the flowing lines of the bed-hangings, echoed by the line of the curtains which softly filter the light. A green moiré print, popular during this period, is used for the bedspread, edged in burgundy braid which also defines the Empire-style bolsters. The sleigh bed and the two chairs have the flowing curves of the period. The green moiré print is picked up in the upholstery as well as the wall covering.

LEFT BELOW The same room is given a less grand, though equally feminine feel with a floral chintz used for both curtains and canopy, draped in a more casual style.

An Edwardian Bedroom

An informal elegance and richness were the stylistic criteria of the Edwardian era. Edward VII himself filled the royal residence at Sandringham with comfortable furniture covered in warm, masculine patterns. This desire for comfort is as prevalent today, as is the delight that the Edwardians took in fabric, pattern, textures and trimmings.

The confidently masculine mood of the time is evoked here in the strong tones of burgundy, navy and tan. Handsome stripes lend rigour to the scheme, while the well-worn leather luggage and the sporting prints create an atmosphere that is agreeably reminiscent of the traditional Gentleman's Club.

RIGHT The same paisley pattern is used in a different combination of the same colours in another Edwardian master-bedroom, this time in conjunction with a wallpaper striped with a pattern of oakleaves to create a still more densely lavish effect.

BELOW RIGHT Well-chosen details such as the popular cut-out silhouette pictures, an antique tapestry bell-pull and the congenial clutter of a masculine dressing-table add to the richly venerable period feel.

Sources of the Style

... the hanging [of] uniform purple paper [are] hung all over with the court of Henry ye 8th. copied after the Holbeins in the Queen's closet at Kensington, in black and gold frame. The bed is either to be from Burleigh (the Lord Exeter is new furnishing it, and means to sell some of his old household stuff) of the rich old tarnished embroidery, or if that is not to be had, and it must be new, it is to be a cut velvet with a dark purple pattern in a stone-colour satin ground, and deep mixt fringes and tassels.

Thomas Gray

So Thomas Gray, the eighteenth-century poet, writes excitedly in a letter about the creation of one of the most famous period bedrooms of all, the Holbein Chamber of Horace Walpole, who obviously had immense fun tracking down both 'authentic' and suitably atmospheric pieces for his new creation. As Walpole shows, period style has the distinction of being both a critical discipline and a work of the imagination. You need to learn about the period, but at the same time you have to re-create it out of what is available, using imagination to fill the gaps.

The past has been a constant source of ideas from the fifteenth century to the present day. The Renaissance saw a huge resurgence of interest in the Classical arts, an influence which affected architecture and interiors all over Europe, and led eventually to the caryatids and columns on Elizabethan chests and beds. Lack of accurate information was a problem then; there were no photographs and few books, so Classical forms were not always resuscitated in the purest way (in England, not until Inigo Jones went to Italy to see for himself). But as an influence it lasted into the eighteenth century when, at the same time that Walpole was inaugurating the fashion for the Gothic picturesque, the rediscovery of the ruins of Herculaneum and Pompeii led to a renewed interest in Classical decoration. The latter half of the eighteenth century saw the Greek Revival, and the genuine re-creation of Classical rooms in domestic houses – in effect, period style. By the 1840s the Gothic style was back in fashion, this time re-interpreted in high moral tones, a far cry from Walpole's fanciful fondness for the picturesque.

Rampant 'period' style, embracing practically every possible period, was the rage on both sides of the Channel, and indeed on both sides of the Atlantic as well. In London, Arrowsmiths, the Queen's decorators, sub-titled their *Home Decorator's and Painter's Guide* as 'suited to the various styles of architecture ... Greek, Roman, Arabesque, Pompeiian, Gothic, Cinque Cento, François Premier, and the more modern French'.

Today, the new passion for the past has brought in its wake much more information and knowledge than was available to decorators of previous

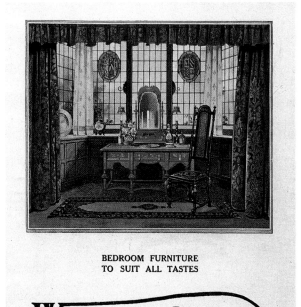

BEDROOM FURNITURE
TO SUIT ALL TASTES

WARING & GILLOW LTD

Furnishers & Decorators to H.M. the King.

164-180 OXFORD STREET, LONDON, W. 1.

Telephone: MUSEUM 5000   Telegrams: "WARISON, LONDON"

BOLD STREET, LIVERPOOL   **DEANSGATE, MANCHESTER**

A Waring & Gillow scheme for a bedroom, dated 1917. They claimed to produce 'bedroom furniture to suit all tastes', in this case a dressing-table in Elizabethan style.

A mid-Victorian bedroom, depicted by Richard Redgrave, shows the use of a decorative screen to separate the dressing area. It is covered in the same richly patterned fabric as the walls, and the carpet increases the sense of pattern laid upon pattern. The dressing-table is a Victorian reproduction in Louis XV style, characterized by its curved form and gilt decoration.

centuries. Books, photographs and magazines are devoted to period interiors, houses from the cottage to the country house are open to the public, bodies like the Georgian Society and the Victorian Society promote interest in every aspect of period life, museums too exhibit carefully re-created interiors of different eras with historical exactitude. In order to evoke the mood of another time, use should be made of all these excellent sources and also this wealth of contemporaneous images.

Creating a Period Bedroom

WALLPAPER, FABRIC, PAINT AND DECORATIVE DETAILS

Illusion is the essence of period style, and it is the background to the period bedroom – the choice of colours, wallpapers and furnishing fabrics -- that allows you to conjure up a Tudor bedchamber or a Rococo boudoir in a modern home. Laura Ashley fabric and wallpaper collections are particularly strong in the patterns of the mid-eighteenth to mid-nineteenth centuries, but the span is much broader than that from medieval flamestitch and bargello patterns that would happily grace a fifteenth-century bedroom to the bold, figurative splashes of Bloomsbury designs, created by Duncan Grant and Vanessa Bell in the 1930s. Period fabrics have been taken principally from nineteenth-century chintzes, and furnishing and dress cottons, but also from sources like the Bradford Table Carpet (a famous sixteenth-century tapestry), early Georgian damasks, French mid-eighteenth-century woven silks and centuries-old stamped velvets.

Increasingly, paintings and prints yield wonderful pattern ideas for the period bedroom. A striped wallpaper derives from a late eighteenth-century mezzotint, for example. Other patterns derive from even more eclectic sources such as trunk linings, a Victorian curtain valance found in an antique shop, or a needlework cushion – all can provide inspiration for the period bedroom.

The type of fabrics used at certain periods is also an important consideration. Satin-weave cotton, for example, is the equivalent of the nineteenth-century cotton sateen which upholstered many drawing rooms. With its smooth, satin sheen and softer draping abilities, it is ideal for the bed hangings and window drapery in a Victorian bedroom. Beds and upholstery of earlier periods used silks and satins, too, and satin-weave cotton will give the equivalent sense of sumptuous softness. The dobby-weave has its roots in the eighteenth century. A more hardwearing cloth, its application would be for upholstery.

Fabrics are mellowed by centuries of light and use which gives them a genuine and characterful look. A collection inspired by Venetian gold-dappled velvets and brocades has been treated with a new process which variegates the background and dulls and flakes the gold in patches to give a venerable feel. This effect has long been prized by decorators of period rooms (Thomas Gray speaks approvingly of Walpole's 'tarnished gold' bed trimmings), and gives a newly arranged room the feeling of having been lived in for years.

Learning to adapt is the secret of counterfeiting a room of another period. An absence of cornices can be overcome by using a paper border to edge the walls above and below, at skirting level and to mark a dado area. Flush modern doors can be transformed by beading (always remember that the top and bottom

TOP *The Bradford Table Carpet (sixteenth-century) is worked in silk, its centre a pattern of vine leaves and grapes, while the elaborate borders are alive with country scenes.*

ABOVE *Its modern-day facsimile brings a period touch to any bedroom.*

The decorative use of pictures can establish a distinctive period feel. A late eighteenth-century fashion was to hang small prints from long lengths of velvet ribbon tied into a bow at the top, usually as a pair flanking some other picture or decorative object. In fact, paintings were not always hung with their cords hidden, or even with frames. They were often hung from great tafetta bows or from simple decorative cords of black twisted satin rope. For the Victorians, grouping was all. Sometimes pictures were hung asymmetrically but densely in an assortment of shapes and sizes, but usually order was sought. Size and shape rather than subject or style dictated the arrangement.

panels of old doors are rarely equal in height), and beautiful old door fittings. Areas of plate glass look very much of the twentieth century, but these can be effectively disguised by a panel of lace. The shape of a window can be visually altered by hanging curtains and valances to suggest that it is taller or wider. The style of curtain treatment, the type of valance as well as the fabrics used, make an instant statement. Period upholsterer's guides can provide valuable ideas for pelmet and curtain designs.

Floors are another consideration. Though they were left bare at many periods throughout history, an unobtrusive fitted carpet can be used as a compromise between period authenticity and comfort. The earliest kind of fitted matting dates from the early seventeenth century, and fitted pile carpets with borders appeared in the eighteenth century. Reproductions are not limited to wallpapers and fabrics. Carpets from the early nineteenth century have been reproduced in Brussels weave, as well as abstract rugs designed in the 1930s.

Details are important in a period bedroom. Individual objects which speak strongly of a certain era help the untrained eye to identify the style of the room. A washstand with its jug and basin instantly recalls Victorian style whereas delicate china, depicting *putti* or dimpling shepherdesses, recalls the mid-eighteenth century. It is these key objects, so characteristic of a period, which unconsciously create an authentic period ambience. You can then begin to add touches which are less characteristic, though they may be equally authentic, and this will give more subtlety to the whole.

Lighting is often overlooked: a bedroom can be given a more genuine flavour with period lamps and candlestands, fitted to take electricity if you prefer, though nothing evokes the past more than candlelight. Chandeliers are best adapted to electricity, their electric cords mitigated by a sock of pretty fabric to match the room. Little china candlesticks with handles for carrying upstairs will usually look Victorian though you can still buy them today. A tall, attenuated candlestand will impart an Empire atmosphere, but its effect will be much increased if you have a *pair* of them, and stand them on either side of a bed or a mirror in perfect symmetry.

The hanging of pictures is another key to the period. Every age had its characteristic approach to picture hanging from the seventeenth-century method of nailing portraits blithely through expensive tapestries without much thought for symmetry or fabric, to the floor-to-ceiling approach of the early-eighteenth-century gallery, or the double and treble hanging schemes of the Victorians.

Furniture for a Period Bedroom

If you can afford a complete set of furniture from the period you have chosen, and have the eye and knowledge to put this together well, then the problem of period furniture is solved for you. Otherwise, ingenuity is needed. A Georgian room, for example, can be decorated to take the less costly, country Georgian style of furniture, which is still well-made and elegant. And the Victorian copies which abound, or good, modern reproductions, distressed to show signs of age, will simulate even an Elizabethan bedroom.

A typical or instantly recognizable period piece will do much to give the bedroom the right feel, even if the rest of the furniture is fairly undistinctive. A set of seventeenth-century bed-steps, perhaps, or an eighteenth-century night-table complete with chamberpot. This sort of furniture suggests the way the bedroom was *used* as much as how it looked. Similarly, in a Victorian re-creation, a plump chaise longue is a vivid reminder of the time, while in a Rococo room a frothy dressing-table or a curvaceous *escritoire*, painted with ribbons or *putti*, perfectly captures the look. An accurate period impression can be summoned with key objects like a screen, which gives an eighteenth- or nineteenth-century feel, depending on what it is covered with, its outline and how it is used – to screen a fire perhaps, or a corner of the room which is being used for tea or for dressing, or to fill a corner decoratively, perhaps in conjunction with a table holding pots of Victorian plants.

Upholstery is a useful tool in giving a piece of furniture a decidedly period cast, and it can be changed easily and inexpensively using reproduction period fabrics. Positioning is also important, and a simple move like taking the furniture and chairs back against the walls with the bed-head in the centre of one wall will suggest something before the mid-eighteenth century.

Something as ubiquitous in the contemporary bedroom as a wardrobe was not always part of a period bedroom. The humbler Tudor household had a recess in the thickly-plastered walls where clothes were stored behind a protective and decorative curtain. Later, large presses and wardrobes stood outside on the landing where their monumental stance looked imposing. The eighteenth-century French style can be evoked with an *armoire*, a particularly elegant form of wardrobe quite different to the solid English version, often beautifully carved and with pleated silk hung in place of panels of wood in the doors.

But one of the most creative ways of putting together a period bedroom requires no more than a good eye. Horace Walpole unwittingly exercised this principle when he picked up at auction a set of chairs and a table for his Holbein bedroom at Strawberry Hill. He and his friends thought they were Tudor – in fact they were seventeenth-century and from the East Indies – but the important thing was that they spelt 'Gothic' to them.

The elegant curves of this Victorian mahogany chaise longue give an immediate period feel. Facsimile fabrics of different eras reinforce the effect. This reproduction flamestitch pattern is edged in sage braid, while the tailored bolster is given definition by a neatly piped border, set off by a typical Victorian trimming – a thick tassel.

The Period Bed

The thrill of sleeping in a period bedroom restored by a knowing and loving hand is recorded by James Lees-Milne, pioneer of the British National Trust, in *Ancestral Voices*:

Ted had given me the North Room next to the Parlour, the room with a double bed and original blue-green and white crewel-work hangings . . . I lay in bed with one candle guttering behind a glass hurricane globe (for there is no electric light in the house) and the logs' flickering thin flames felt rather than seen through the half-drawn bed curtains . . .

He picks up on the things that give period atmosphere to the bedroom. A candle and a real fire in place of artificial light and heat can provide an atmospheric and dramatic element. Other than that, it is, of course, the bed that is most important. But what is particularly interesting here is that it is the bed *hangings* rather than the bedstead itself which gives a sense of the past. In fact, a simple, modern four-poster frame can be transformed with just one element – fabric. The most basic support can be artfully disguised with drapery according to the style of the period.

Fabric has been the principle method of dressing up the bed, of giving it a particular style, since the thirteenth century. The eighteenth century saw a proliferation of different styles of bed which were often no more than the same bed with different hangings. So a simple sleigh bed, for example, became a *lit à la polonaise* with curtains suspended from a ceiling mounted corona, or a *couronne* bed with a canopy suspended from a corona attached to the wall behind. Placed in a shallow alcove, sideways to the wall with decorative hangings in front, it became a *lit en niche*. All these can be easily re-created.

Not all period beds are hard to find, however. Splendid Victorian brass beds can be picked up in antique shops and also beautiful French beds of the nineteenth and early twentieth centuries, often with interesting headboards. Colonial beds, popular in Edwardian and Victorian days, often have great charm, sometimes with panels of rattan or carved posts of richly-coloured and grained tropical woods.

A simple iron bed, given a coat of crisp white paint, is transformed by the addition of a simple four-poster frame into a Victorian bedstead. The bed hangings are of simple cotton, lightly sprigged in the early Victorian manner, and match the quilted bedspread and curtains, which are given the same loose, box-pleated treatment. A complementary print lines the bed hangings, and the whole room is set off with such details as the typical jug and basin, and a slipper chair.

THE TOWN BEDROOM

And in her bedroom, a cool room which got the morning sun only ... she would dress herself carefully and brush her hair ... Sometimes it was still light when she went to bed, but as the light was of such very great interest to her she would put down her book to watch it fade, and change colour ... Her bed was white and plain and not quite big enough.
Anita Brookner, *Hotel du Lac*, 1984

What is Town Style?

Town style is completely cosmopolitan and international. The elements are the same on either side of the Atlantic or indeed either side of the world. It is easy to live with, yet experimental. The style has an urbane edge to it – tautness, a certain pace, smart and upbeat. Colours are used either as a bold statement or as subtle background. Patterns are stylized repeat shapes used with graphic boldness or in lighter, regularly-stamped designs. Town bedrooms are unfussy with an atmosphere of balance and cool composure, where design acts as a counterpoint to decoration. The result is poise.

A town bedroom, whilst drawing on the fund of ideas from past eras, maintains a sense of timelessness in which no one period is allowed to dominate the mood. Period objects, when taken out of context, reveal different sides to their characters. Classical and architectural motifs work strikingly well in modern interiors. The traditional patchwork quilt, for example, can look strong and geometric in such a setting; garden statuary can bring a witty sculptural element, and a gilded period chair will look even more distinctive against a spartan background. The past is made to look contemporary, not the other way round. In fact, a room looks even more contemporary when this eclectic touch is added than when its modern character is left unchallenged.

TOP *A spartan sophistication and air of uncluttered ease marks this town bedroom with its bare, gleaming floorboards and the graphic line of the wrought-iron bedstead.*

LEFT *A small town bedroom is given a touch of period grandeur with contrasting fabrics used to drape the window and frame the bedhead. Bright, bold stripes give an instantly up-to-date look.*

RIGHT *The purist's bedroom and living room rolled into one. In spite of its magnificent bareness, it has all the elements of eclecticism: a grand piano, 'Corinthian' columns, a Japanese-style flower arrangement. Yet they work harmoniously together. The bed is drawn right into the middle of the room, and its downy softness and lightly-stippled pattern are in pleasing contrast to the room's sharp edges.*

The Classic Town Bedroom

One of the problems common in city life is that of space. Often the bedroom is forced to merge with the living room. This is a challenge to any designer. However, many houses of the eighteenth and nineteenth centuries, now divided up into studio apartments, have ample ceiling height to accommodate a split level, and a gallery is often the happiest way of making a virtue of a necessity.

RIGHT This spacious studio room is divided into three spaces: the main living area, the sleeping area on a platform above, and a more intimate eating area below. A background of stripes and cool blocks of colour in grey and apricot hold these various elements together.

LEFT, TOP An accessory of some antiquity, but both decorative and useful in the town bedroom, is the screen. Totally versatile, its style is dependent on its covering and shape. As a room divider, it has flexibility – it can be re-arranged or removed altogether (here, it serves as a space-saving doorway).

LEFT, CENTRE The decoration is a marvellous balance between the restfulness of softly coloured bare walls and the breezy insouciance of Duncan Grant's ebullient prints.

LEFT, BELOW The window treatment has a period derivation, yet is entirely of the present. Instead of fringes, blinds can be edged in webbing, perhaps with an elegant detail along the top. Where period festoons might have had a pelmet of choux and swags, the same idea can be translated into a line of twisted rope, knotted to each side and in the centre.

Sources of the Style

The 1980s have seen a new sophistication in town style. The brash exuberance of the 1960s has been replaced by a more subtle sensibility, and a more objective appraisal of the past has replaced the nostalgia of the 1970s. The sources for a town bedroom range from a stark, Corbusier-style interior to a country-house bedroom designed by John Fowler – perhaps a combination of the two. Period pieces, borrowings from abroad or from nature, are taken out of context and set into a background of simple good taste. The result is something more than the sum of its parts.

A glance at the changes being wrought in architecture throws light on *interior* decoration. Modernism is no longer the only style for a contemporary environment. Now, the Classical orders of architecture are being re-invented with a fresh eye. At the same time, architects are taking a more playful look at eclecticism, juggling a motif from one style with the lines of another, blocks of bright colour here with the natural texture of stone there to express a new feeling of wit and vigour. This trend has permeated interiors as well as exteriors. There is the same logical leaning towards the clean, simple, Classical shapes against a modern background, rooms in which architectural features are emphasized, and where furniture is an essential part of the composition.

ABOVE The 1970s saw a nostalgic revival of interest in the rustic tradition and the use of natural materials. Pale, muted colours were a reaction against the strident interiors of the 1960s; yet the long, low lines of this wicker daybed, the space-saving answer to the small dimensions of the town apartment, still have a modern profile.

RIGHT This bedroom, designed by the Post-modernist architect Charles Jencks, draws on the classical tradition whilst at the same time incorporating a witty eclecticism in the 'gothic' detailing of the bed. Cruciform in shape, the bedroom is flooded with light from a skylight set directly above the bed.

Creating a Town Bedroom

WALLPAPER, FABRIC, PAINT AND DECORATIVE DETAILS

There is a feeling of coolness in the town bedroom. It is crisp, assured and smart, bringing with it a sense of space. Walls are usually uncluttered zones that open up the room. Subtlety and a sense of texture come from paint effects – stippling, dragging, or lightly sponging one shade of colour over another: jade with pale jade; coral and terracotta; or rose and plum. There are more emphatic paint effects, too, such as distressing, marbling and graining, ideas culled from eighteenth-century country houses.

When wallpaper is used it tends to be unobtrusive, an abstract pattern that looks more like broken colour than repeat-patterned wallpaper. The alternative is simple, strong, geometric patterns or stripes, either broad and subtle, perhaps in dark cream alternating with pale ivory, or narrower and sharper, with the tonic effect of blue and white, or the modernist's favourite of black-and-white liquorice striping.

TOP A new sensitivity to architectural features is an important aspect of today's approach to the town house. While previous decades have tended to remove or obscure decorative plaster mouldings, modern decorators make the most of their charms.

ABOVE A blue and white town bedroom takes its colour scheme from Chinese porcelain. The marbled floor conjures up a feeling of coolness, while the mirrored walls create an illusion of space – a real bonus in today's sometimes cramped surroundings.

A floor of marbelized tiles does as much to draw a draught of coolness into the bedroom as anything else. It is an idea gleaned from Italian *palazzi*, but transformed by a modern setting. Floors might be painted and stencilled in simplified imitation of some marvellous floor glimpsed in a country house or on the Continent. They might be covered with simple, neutral rush or coir matting, left plain or with one or two beautiful rugs. Bare boards, too, dry-scrubbed in the eighteenth-century manner, have a well-seasoned softness that sets off the faded colours of antique carpets more subtly than wax or polish. Yet a bedroom can gain a sophisticated elegance from a dancing-floor of sleek, waxed boards. Wax brings out the golden tones in the wood and gives a sheen that reflects the clean finish of a room. A quiet-coloured fitted carpet has the same effect as matting, with less texture. It is the most unobtrusive, almost hushed, grounding for a town bedroom.

A renewed feel for pattern, for fabric and for texture means that more prints are being used together with solid colour. Very stylized rustic sprigs look chic when used in conjunction with a more sophisticated pattern like stripes, and their scale means that they do not compete with each other. There is a growing phalanx of figurative designs, inspired by the past, and not always the distant past, that have the freshness of colour and lightness of touch to enable them to be used extensively in a town bedroom without overpowering it.

The architectural features of a period house can be an advantage to a town bedroom. Period fireplaces, cornices, dados and shutters are nearly always left *in situ* now, adding their authenticity to the bedroom's mellow, eclectic mood.

ABOVE A streamlined look is the essence of urban chic: sleek roller blinds and lamps with a Classical profile sum it up.

BELOW A decorative border used at dado level and taken over the door frame is echoed by the low lines of this simple wooden couch with its gingham-covered cushion.

Windows are often treated with great simplicity in a way which will show off their architectural bones. Light is one of the most covetable elements in a town bedroom and windows can be left completely bare, or given festoon blinds which do not obscure their shape.

Decorative valances and curtains, of the Regency period in particular, are a source increasingly plundered for urban windows. A window treatment might be of striped fabric exactly matching the wallpaper, no more than a valance dipped into a swag with long tails thrown over at either side, falling in zigzags which are outlined with a stylized border. Curtains can also be used alone, suspended from a plain pole and perhaps drawn back by the simplest tie-backs. Shutters have the simplicity of the perfect city backdrop.

Finishing touches can make all the difference between blandness and the sharply, but informally, delineated edge that is the essence of town style. Borders, for example, are used to give a more emphatic line and shape to the room. The strong outline of a window can be brought sharply into focus, or the juxtaposition of wall and skirting board pointed up in the same way. The clean-cut lines of picture frames repeat the effect. Plants are often used as elements of design, and the sculptural shapes of greenery rather than flowers work well in the town bedroom. Cushions and pillows, neatly piped in a contrasting colour, bring out a graphic edge. Objects should be striking, but few, so as to acquire an almost sculptural quality.

In the town bedroom it is the decorative objects which carry the impact of the room and make the most emphatic statements about its character.

Furniture for a Town Bedroom

Usually, there is not a great deal of furniture in a town bedroom. Sometimes it is a deliberate act of stripping bare. There is a great sense of luxury in this feeling of spaciousness. More often, a minimal approach to furniture stems from a need for comfort without clutter. Many town bedrooms have to be clever enough to act as a sitting room, dining room and baby's bedroom as well.

Several kinds of furniture might suit a town bedroom. The first is that easy, unobtrusive, modern style of seating – the long, low sofa, which always has a strong sense of the horizontal and takes up little visual space. Certain pieces of country furniture, such as upright wooden chairs or long, low chests of drawers work well; their simplicity blends with the clean-cut urban mood.

Placing period furniture against a decidedly urbane backdrop tends to add more interest and depth to a town bedroom. The lyrical arabesques of a nineteenth-century chair back are beautifully set off by a spare, sophisticated context. Gryphons, masks and gilding simply look amusing and sculptural when juxtaposed with a muted but sophisticated bedroom. The secret is not to have too many period pieces but to leaven them by mingling periods and adding unpretentious modern touches.

There are, of course, some very fine pieces of modern furniture being made that work beautifully in the town bedroom. Modern furniture tends to be plain and smooth with very little surface decoration, and, apart from upholstery, little colour. It is about sketched outlines or solid, simple shapes meant to show off the beauty of texture and grain with no further adornment. Their simplicity evokes a sense of serenity.

The Town Bed

One way of maximising space in the town bedroom is to camouflage the bed as a sofa. It may seem an entirely new idea, evolved specifically to cope with the city squeeze, but like almost everything else, it has a long history. In 1644 the diarist John Evelyn noted two 'conceited chayres' at Rome which converted into 'a bed, a bolster, a table, a couch' – even more flexible than the simple sofa-bed.

Many town beds are no more than a streamlined divan. Covered with a quilt piled high with pillows, it becomes an oasis of comfort. But while the simple divan continues to be popular, many city bedrooms are exploring the new possibilities of the highly decorative beds of the past. More and more Empire and Biedermeier beds in particular are being used in non-period settings. They have the feel for line and tautness which connect with this same spirit in modern settings. Colonial beds, too, made to do service for the British Empire, often have a modern edge, with low-relief carving set off with panels of rattan in the head- and footboards.

But perhaps the most interesting development of the town bed is the growing use of canopies. Perennially popular for four-posters, both in the country and in period bedrooms, it is only now that we are developing an eye for what canopies can add to the town bedroom. A triangular-shaped canopy, suspended from a short gilt curtain post above and caught back at the sides by two others to give it a slight swag, creates the right feel. Lined in a contrasting fabric, with perhaps a fan of gathered pleats, its rustic candour becomes sophistication. Canopies in this kind of bedroom tend to have a well-judged effect that is neither 'masculine' nor 'feminine' but a chic stroke of simplicity. When taking inspiration for a town bedroom from canopies in a country house or in a period painting, extract the essence of the idea, pare it of elaboration and execute a simple and elegant version which will look unaffected and at home.

The strong individual character of the colonial bed, with its carved mahogany foot- and headboard infilled with latticed rattan, has an appropriate modern edge to it.

LAURA ASHLEY SHOPS

In addition there are a further 297 retail outlets in the United Kingdom, Europe and the Pacific Basin.

CANADA

Sherway Gardens,
ETOBICOKE,
Ontario,
M9C 1B2

2110 Crescent Street,
MONTREAL,
Quebec,
H3G 2B8

136 Bank Street,
OTTAWA,
Ontario,
K1P 5N8

2452 Wilfred Laurier
Boulevard,
STE-FOY,
Quebec,
G1V 2L1

18 Hazelton Avenue,
TORONTO,
Ontario,
M5R 2E2

1171 Robson Street,
VANCOUVER,
British Columbia,
V6E 1B5

Bayview Village Shopping
Center,
2901 Bayview Avenue,
WILLOWDALE,
Ontario,
M2K 1E6

Mail order:

Laura Ashley,
5165 Sherbrook Street W.,
Suite 124,
MONTREAL,
Quebec,
H4A 1T6

UNITED STATES

Crossgates Mall,
120 Washington Avenue
Extension,
ALBANY, NY 12203

139 Main Street,
ANNAPOLIS, MD 21401

514 East Washington Street,
ANN ARBOR, MI 48104

29 Surburban Square,
ARDMORE, PA 19003

Lenox Square,
3393 Peachtree Road,
ATLANTA, GA 30326

Perimeter Mall,
4400 Ashford-Dunwoody
Road,
ATLANTA, GA 30346

Highland Mall 1224,
6001 Airport Boulevard,
AUSTIN, TX 78752

Pratt Street Pavilion,
Harborplace,
BALTIMORE, MD 21202

203 Beachwood Place,
26300 Cedar Road,
BEACHWOOD, OH 44122

200–219 Riverchase
Galleria Mall,
BIRMINGHAM, AL 35244

180 Town Center Mall,
BOCA RATON, FL 33431

83 Newbury Street,
BOSTON, MA 02116

23 Church Street,
BURLINGTON, VT 05401

Charles Square,
5 Bennett Street,
CAMBRIDGE, MA 02138

Carmel Plaza,
CARMEL-BY-THE-SEA,
CA 93921

Charleston Place,
130 Market Street,
CHARLESTON, SC 29401

The Mall at Chesnut Hill,
199 Boylston Street,
CHESNUT HILL, MA 02167

Watertower Place,
835 N. Michigan Avenue,
CHICAGO, IL 60611

The Citadel,
750 Citadel Drive E. 2008,
COLORADO SPRINGS,
CO 80909

1636 Redwood Highway,
CORTE MADERA, CA 94925

3333 Bristol Street,
South Coast Plaza,
COSTA MESA, CA 92629

Galleria 13350 Dallas
Parkway,
Suite 1585,
DALLAS, TX 75240

423 North Park Center,
DALLAS, TX 75225

Danbury Fair Mall C-118,
7 Backus Avenue,
DANBURY, CT 06810

1439 Larimer Street,
DENVER, CO 80202

The Kaleidoscope at the Hub,
555 Walnut Street,
Suite 218,
DES MOINES, IA 50309

Twelve Oaks Mall,
27498 Novi Road,
Suite A,
DETROIT, MI 48056

Galleria Shopping Center,
3505 West 69th Street,
EDINA, MN 55435

11822 Fair Oaks Mall,
FAIRFAX, VA 22033

West Farms Mall,
FARMINGTON, CT 06032

2492 E. Sunrise Boulevard,
Galleria Mall,
FORT LAUDERDALE,
FL 33304

213 Hulen Mall,
FORT WORTH, TX 76132

58 Main Street,
FREEPORT, ME 04032

Saddle Creek Shopping
Center,
7615 W. Farmington
Boulevard,
GERMANTON, 38138

Glendale Galleria,
GLENDALE, CA 91210

Woodland Mall,
3175 28th Street S.E.,
GRAND RAPIDS, MI 49508

321 Greenwich Avenue,
GREENWICH, CT 06830

Riverside Square Mall,
HACKENSACK, NJ 07601

Ala Moana Center 2246,
HONOLULU, HI 96814

The Galleria,
5015 Westheimer,
Suite 2120,
HOUSTON, TX 77056

1000 West Oaks Mall,
Suite 124,
HOUSTON, TX 77082

Fashion Mall,
8702 Keystone Crossing,
INDIANAPOLIS, IN 46240

The Jacksonville Landing,
2 Independent Drive,
JACKSONVILLE, FL 32202

Country Club Plaza,
308 W. 47th Street,
KANSAS CITY, MO 64112

The Esplanade,
1401 W. Esplanade,
KENNER, LA 70065

White Flint Shopping Mall,
11301 Rockville Pike,
KENSINGSTON, MD 20895

7852 Girard Avenue,
LA JOLLA, CA 92037

Pavilion in the Park,
8201 Cantrell Road,
LITTLE ROCK, AR 72207

10250 Santa Monica
Boulevard,
LOS ANGELES, CA 90067

Beverly Center,
121 N. La Cienaga Boulevard,
Suite 739,
LOS ANGELES, CA 90048

Louisville Galleria 109,
LOUISVILLE, KY 40202

2042 Northern Boulevard,
Americana Shopping Center,
MANHASSET, NY 11030

Tysons Corner Center,
1961 Chain Bridge Road,
MCLEAN, VA 22102

The Falls,
Space 373,
8888 Howard Drive,
MIAMI, FL 33176

The Grand Avenue,
275 W. Wisconsin Avenue 5,
MILWAUKEE, WI 53203

208 City Center,
40 South 7th Street,
MINNEAPOLIS, MN 55402

Ridgedale Center,
12401 Wayzota Boulevard,
MINNETONKA, MN 55343

The Mall at Green Hills,
2148 Abbot Martin Road,
NASHVILLE, TN 37215

260–262 College Street,
NEW HAVEN, CT 06510

333 Canal Street,
151 Canal Place,
NEW ORLEANS, LA 70130

979 3rd Avenue,
NEW YORK, NY 10022
(Decorator Showroom)

398 Columbus Avenue,
NEW YORK, NY 10024

4 Fulton Street,
NEW YORK, NY 10038

21 East 57th Street,
NEW YORK, NY 10021

2164 Northbrook Court,
NORTHBROOK, IL 60062

224 Oakbrook Center,
OAKBROOK, IL 60521

Owings Mills Town Center,
10300 Mill Run Circle 1062,
OWINGS MILLS, MD 21117

320 Worth Avenue,
PALM BEACH, FL 33480

469 Desert Fashion Plaza,
123 North Palm Canyon
  Drive,
PALM SPRINGS, CA 92262

12 Stanford Shopping
  Center,
PALO ALTO, CA 94304

221 Paramus Park,
Route 17,
PARAMUS, NJ 07652

401 South Lake Avenue,
PASADENA, CA 91101

1721 Walnut Street,
PHILADELPHIA, PA 19103

Biltmore Fashion Park,
2478 E. Camelback Road,
PHOENIX, AZ 85016

20 Commerce Court,
Station Square,
PITTSBURGH, PA 15219

1000 Ross Park Mall,
PITTSBURGH, PA 15237

2100 Collin Creek Mall,
811 No. Central Expressway,
PLANO, TX 75075

419 S.W. Morrison Street,
PORTLAND, OR 97204

46 Nassau Street,
Palmer Square,
PRINCETON, NJ 08544

2 Davol Square Mall,
Point & Eddy Street,
PROVIDENCE, RI 02903

Crabtree Valley Mall,
4325 Glenwood Avenue,
RALEIGH, NC 27612

South Bay Galleria,
1815 Hawthorne Boulevard,
Space 172,
REDONDO BEACH, CA 90278

Commercial Block,
1217 E. Cary Street,
RICHMOND, VA 23219

Regency Square Mall,
1404 Parham Road,
RICHMOND, VA 23229

Northpark Mall,
1200 East County Line Road,
RIDGELAND, MI 39157

531 Pavilions Lane,
SACRAMENTO, CA 95825

74 Plaza Frontenac,
ST LOUIS, MO 63131

St Louis Center C-330
515N. 6th Street,
ST LOUIS, MO 63101

Trolley Square,
SALT LAKE CITY, UT 84102

247 Horton Plaza,
Space 265,
SAN DIEGO, CA 92101

University Town Center,
SAN DIEGO, CA 92122

1827 Union Street,
SAN FRANCISCO, CA 94123

563 Sutter Street,
SAN FRANCISCO, CA 94102
(Decorator Showroom)

Suite 1224,
North Star Mall,
7400 SAN PEDRO,
San Antonio, TX 78216

Le Cumba Galleria,
3891 State Street 109,
SANTA BARBARA, CA 93105

Valley Fair Mall,
Suite 1031,
2855 Stevens Creek
  Boulevard,
SANTA CLARA, CA 95050

696 White Plains Road,
SCARSDALE, NY 10583

F-331 Woodfield Mall,
SCHAUMBURG, IL 60173

405 University Street,
SEATTLE, DC 98101

The Mall at Short Hills,
SHORT HILLS, NJ 07078

20 Old Orchard Shopping
  Center,
SKOKIE, IL 60077

Stamford Town Center,
100 Greyrock Place,
STAMFORD, CT 06902

139 Main Street,
STONY BROOK, NY 11790

Old Hyde Park Village,
718 S. Village Circle,
TAMPA, FL 33606

2845 Somerset Mall,
TROY, MI 48084

Utica Square,
1846 21 Street,
TULSA, OK 74114

1171 Broadway Plaza,
WALNUT CREEK, CA 94596

300 D Street SW,
Washington, DC 20024
(Decorator Showroom)

3213 M. Street NW,
Georgetown,
WASHINGTON, DC 20007

85 Main Street,
WESTPORT, CT 06880

Bullocks Westwood Shops,
10861 Weyburn Avenue,
WESTWOOD, CA 90025

422 Duke of Gloucester
  Street,
WILLIAMSBURG, VA 23185

290 Park Avenue North,
WINTER PARK,
FL 32789

740 Hanes Mall,
WINSTON-SALEM, NC 27103

279 Promenade Mall,
WOODLAND HILLS, CA 91367

108 Worthington Square
  Mall,
WORTHINGTON, OH 43085

Mail order:

Laura Ashley Inc.,
1300 MacArthur Boulevard,
MAHWAH, NJ 07430

BIBLIOGRAPHY

Fowler, John and Cornforth, John, *English Decoration in the Eighteenth Century*, Barrie & Jenkins, 1974

Gray, Cecil and Margery, *The Bed*, Nicholson & Watson, 1946

Harris, Eileen, *Going to Bed*, Victoria & Albert Museum, 1981

Jackson-Stops, Gervase, *The English Country House: A Grand Tour*, The National Trust/Weidenfeld & Nicolson, 1985

Thornton, Peter, *Authentic Decor: The Domestic Interior 1620–1920*, Weidenfeld & Nicolson, 1984

ACKNOWLEDGMENTS

All illustrations are reproduced courtesy of the Laura Ashley Archives with the exception of the following:

8/9   Bridgeman Art Library
       Mary Ellen Best, *Bedroom at Langton Hall*, c. 1835

9   Mary Evans Picture Library
       Waring & Gillow design for an Elizabethan bedroom, 1917

10   Ronald Sheridan

11   Victoria & Albert Museum, London

12   Courtesy of Spink & Son Ltd

13   National Trust (photographer: Mark Fiennes)

14   His Grace The Duke of Norfolk, KG

15   Bridgeman Art Library

16   Victoria & Albert Museum, London

17   Victoria & Albert Museum, London/Bridgeman Art Library

19   ABOVE Mary Evans Picture Library
       RIGHT Victoria & Albert Museum, London

22   Mimi Packenham

24   RIGHT Courtesy of Hazlitt, Gooden & Fox

33   ABOVE J. P. Stevens & Co. Inc., New York
       BELOW Syndication International (*Homes & Gardens*)

35   RIGHT J. P. Stevens & Co. Inc., New York

37   Fotobank

38   Elizabeth Whiting & Associates (photographer: David Cripps)

39   Arcaid (photographer: Lucinda Lambton)

40   BELOW Elizabeth Whiting & Associates (photographer: David Cripps)

42   Geffrye Museum

43   ABOVE American Museum in Britain, Bath

44   LEFT Weidenfeld & Nicolson Archives (photographer: Rick Kemp)

47   J. P. Stevens & Co. Inc., New York

48   J. P. Stevens & Co. Inc., New York

50   J. P. Stevens & Co. Inc., New York

51   Weidenfeld & Nicolson Archive (photographer: Robert César)

53   J. P. Stevens & Co. Inc., New York

54   J. P. Stevens & Co. Inc., New York

57   Derry Moore

58   LEFT Victoria & Albert Museum, London
       RIGHT National Trust

62   Arcaid (photographer: Lucinda Lambton)

63   J. P. Stevens & Co. Inc., New York

66   Arcaid (photographer: Lucinda Lambton)

70   Mary Evans Picture Library

71   LEFT National Trust
       RIGHT Victoria & Albert Museum, London

72   LEFT Mary Evans Picture Library
       RIGHT Weidenfeld & Nicolson Archives

74   J. P. Stevens & Co. Inc., New York

77   Arcaid (photographer: Lucinda Lambton)

83   BELOW LEFT National Trust

88   ABOVE LEFT Victoria & Albert Museum, London

90   J. P. Stevens & Co. Inc., New York

92   Mary Evans Picture Library

93   Victoria & Albert Museum, London

94   ABOVE Victoria & Albert Museum, London

98/9   J. P. Stevens & Co. Inc., New York

100   LEFT AND ABOVE J. P. Stevens & Co. Inc., New York

104   RIGHT Elizabeth Whiting & Associates (photographer: Tim Street Porter)

The publishers and Laura Ashley would like to thank David Roos for the designs that appear on pp. 25–29.

GLOSSARY

angel (flying) tester: *see* half-tester.

Arabian bedstead: a half-tester bed popular in Victorian England and reflecting the 19th-century taste for exoticism. Canopies would be heavily draped with fringes and tassels.

bonegrace: a corner bed curtain used in the 17th century for additional draught exclusion, sometimes tied to the side curtains with ribbon bows.

campaign bed: a 19th century, lightweight travelling bed, usually lightly draped with a curved tester.

campane: (Fr.) an inverted box pleat; the valance of a four-poster bed can be pleated in this way with the same treatment used for the window curtains.

chintz: a printed, patterned cotton fabric with a glazed finish.

choux: (Fr., lit. 'cabbages') decorative rosettes of fabric used to garnish the valance of a bed canopy.

colonial bed: a 19th-century bed, often made of tropical woods, with a panel of rattan for the head- and footboards.

corona: a wreath or crown-shaped structure of wood or metal, suspended from the ceiling or attached to the wall, from which drapery is hung to form a canopy around the bedhead.

cornice: a decorative moulding, often carved or painted but sometimes covered in fabric, that edges the tester. From 1780, the cornice could be straight, bowed or serpentine in shape, sometimes with specialised chinoiserie or Gothic detailing according to current fashion.

couronne: (Fr., lit. 'crown') *see* corona.

crewelwork: a popular form of embroidery in the 16th and 17th centuries in England; sewn with loosely twisted, worsted yarn on unbleached cotton or linen.

finial: the terminating ornament on the head- or footposts of a four-poster bed. At various periods, finials were carved in the shape of pineapples, urns or clusters of foliage.

flange: a flat decorative border around a pillow.

flame stitch: a kind of needlework popularly used for bed hangings from the 16th century. Each element of the pattern – usually flame-shaped – is embroidered in a single graduated colour.

four-poster bed: in the Tudor and Elizabethan periods, the four-poster had a panelled headboard, some 7–8 feet high, and 2 footposts, either fixed to the frame or free-standing. These elements supported the canopy or tester. Now, the four-poster bed has literally 'four posts'.

galloon: a narrow, closely-woven braid used for trimming draperies in the 18th century. Galloon of silver and gold lace decorated the state beds.

half-tester: a canopy which covered a quarter to a third of the bed area, supported by headposts only. Known in medieval times, it re-appeared in the 18th and 19th centuries. The angel, or flying, tester was a lighter variant.

lambrequin: a valance board for drapery; often deeply cut to make a decorative silhouette with an arched centre and sides that reached down almost to floor level.

lit à la polonaise: (Fr., lit. 'Polish bed') an 18th-century bed with a sinuous S-shaped frame topped by a small crown canopy. This developed from the hipped testers of Germany and eastern Europe, common in the 17th century.

lit en bateau: (Fr.) a boat-shaped bed of the Empire period.

lit en double tombeau: (Fr.) a bed with a double drape. A length of cloth is hung from a central curtain pole and drifts out over the bed to each side.

moiré: a waved or watered effect on fabric, especially corded silk.

sateen: a cotton fabric with a satin weave, which has a lustrous finish and drapes well. Commonly used in the 19th century for upholstery and curtain drapery.

sparver: a circular canopy or tester over a bed (15th century).

stump bed: used from the 16th century, a wooden bed frame with four short turned or square legs fitted with a plain headboard.

sunburst canopy: a canopy in which the fabric radiates from a central point; originally associated with the style of Louis XIV, the Sun King.

swag: cloth draped in a looped, garlanded effect; used as a decorative element on the valance of bed drapery.

tent bed: an 18th-century variation of the camp or field bed with a light frame and an arched canopy that resembles a bell tent.

tester: originally, the framework for the canopy over a four-poster bed, the tester became a flat wooden structure, panelled and carved. The 17th century saw lighter variants, eg hipped and flying testers, followed by exuberant Baroque testers with carved scrolls which were heavily draped and swathed with fabric. In the mid-18th century, the tester became a wooden cornice with a fabric valance and bed curtains attached. *See* also cornice, valance.

toile: (Fr.) a linen or canvas-like cloth which originated in France. Also, Toile de Jouy, a cotton fabric, most characteristic in pink and white and printed with 18th-century figures and scenes. Such cloth graced the court of Versailles.

trundle or truckle bed: a trundle, or caster, was fitted to a small-scale bed for children or servants. This was rolled under a full-size bed when not in use. It was a feature of the bedchamber from Tudor times.

trussing bed: the practice of moving from one house to another in the 16th and 17th centuries resulted in special trussing or folding beds which could be easily dismantled for travelling.

valance: originally a draught excluder, the valance had the practical function of hiding the structural detail of a canopy. Now it is used decoratively, with fringes and swags.

INDEX

Numbers in *italics* refer to illustration captions